ANTARCTIC DIARY

ANTARCTIC DIARY

A letter to her family

by

MARIA BUXTON

TERENCE DALTON LIMITED
LAVENHAM . SUFFOLK

1983

Published by
TERENCE DALTON LIMITED

ISBN 0 86138 024 X

Text photoset in 11/12pt. Garamond

Printed in Great Britain at
The Lavenham Press Limited, Lavenham, Suffolk

Contents

Index of Illustrations

Foreword

Sir Peter Scott

I AM so pleased to have been asked to contribute a foreword to this lively and delightful account of a visit to Antarctica, the Falkland Islands and South Georgia at a particularly critical and historic period. Maria Buxton's enthusiastic approach to her experiences is expressed with so much freshness and charm. Perhaps the secret of its appeal is that it was written for all the members of her large family. I was myself fascinated when I first read it, and am delighted that it is now available to a wider circle.

With a life-long interest in the Antarctic, which has included five visits to the continent, three of them including the Falkland Islands in the itinerary, I found the book especially absorbing, in particular the accounts of life in the Falkland Islands before the invasion. It is too early to be sure that the way of life which Maria Buxton describes so vividly will once more become normal to the Islanders. I am sure we all hope so. Meanwhile I wish all success to this engaging book.

Peter Scott.

Editor's Introduction

On 20th February, 1982, Maria Buxton left Gatwick Airport with her husband on the first leg of a trip to the Falkland Islands, South Georgia and the Antarctic Peninsula. She was away for five weeks, and during the various landings and the long voyage in H.M.S. *Endurance* wrote a daily "diary" for her large family, seven children and nine grandchildren, which eventually reached them in the form of a long letter.

This has since been read by many friends and relations, and everyone has found it delightful and absorbing, and urged its publication. The author's immediate reaction was that this was out of the question and that such a lighthearted day-to-day account would need complete re-writing, particularly since it was intended only for the family, and some very young ones at that.

But the professional view is that to change it would have altered the entire complexion of a thoroughly readable and charming travel story, with some spice of adventure, and that re-presenting the text with supporting information and expanding all the historical or current background so that it qualified as a "book", in length and style, would have lost far more than might very dubiously have been gained.

Hence Maria Buxton's Antarctic Diary is published here exactly as it was written for the children, mainly on board H.M.S. *Endurance*, strongly complemented by all the photographs taken by herself, by her daughter Cindy, by Annie Price and by a professional photographer, Bob Mahoney, who was on board throughout. The Buxtons were on another tour for Anglia Television, which has made such superb films in the area.

In view of the momentous events which took place afterwards in the South Atlantic, and which for the British public began when scrap-metal merchants arrived in South Georgia on March 20—when the Buxtons were still in the Falklands and had only missed the scrap men by three days—the diary assumes much wider significance and in some instances an unusual dimension. The various experiences and impressions, read now against the background of subsequent events and developments, add much in local colour to the extraordinary and at the time almost unbelievable crop of rumours and straws in the wind which climaxed with the most grotesque, unprovoked invasion of an unprotected peaceful neighbouring country on 2nd April, only a matter of days after the Buxtons had passed through Argentina with some apprehension, to arrive in Rio late at night with relief. It was one thing to be stranded on H.M.S. *Endurance* or in South Georgia, but quite another to be tapped on the shoulder in Buenos Aires and delayed or held without explanation while the preposterous hostilities began. Fortunately nothing happened, as they managed to fly in three hops from Port Stanley to Rio, via Commodoro Rivadavia and Buenos Aires, all in one day. The Argentine Navy was by then "exercising" at sea.

But perhaps of greater interest to readers in this country, now that politicians and public have so suddenly and so rudely been made aware of the Falkland Islanders and their frightful experiences, and the daunting problems and difficulties which they now face, is to read about life as it used to be. The shock experienced by the Islanders, in the violent switch from the traditional peaceful era of a century and a half to the recent chaos and uncertainty, is admirably and instructively demonstrated in the diarist's delightful account of a gymkhana on 24th February, 1982.

This happy gathering took place on the very same peaty soil as the first momentous battles, at Darwin and Goose Green. It is poignant and perhaps traumatic that a visitor from 8,000 miles away should have described with considerable care and detail a conventional social occasion at the very spot where men died to protect such a way of life only a short time afterwards.

Few women from Britain have been fortunate to enjoy such a voyage to the Antarctic with the Royal Navy, and particularly with such a renowned vessel as H.M.S. *Endurance*, which played a vital role in the recapture of South Georgia by the Task Force.

Looking out from the bridge over the bows of *Endurance* in driving snow—a picture which gives some idea of conditions encountered during a patrol in the Antarctic. *Bob Mahoney*

To the Falklands

21st February, 1982

FIRST stop Recife in Brazil, some nine hours away. Rather surprisingly, we were woken at 5 a.m. for tea. Daddy remained asleep, surfacing only when we began to land, looking amazingly like a sleepy Ticket*, asking ''What's going on?'' On being told, went back to sleep. After Recife we were served with a rather delicious breakfast. Quite what the people who boarded at Recife thought of having breakfast at 3 a.m. I can't imagine. There were two of the fattest women I've ever seen came aboard at Recife, they even made me look slim! And they ate a huge breakfast.

From Recife to Rio, then Rio to San Paulo, which I'm told is much the biggest town in Brazil; it looked quite unimpressive from the air, but I'm told it takes four hours to drive from one side to the other. Finally we arrived at Buenos Aires, having by now been served more champagne and a three-course meal (Local time 11 a.m.).

To our surprise we were met by the British Councillor, David Joy, who was charming, and by some miracle all our luggage came off in the first five minutes. We were whizzed through passport control and escaped customs as ''diplomatic'' personnel, which was a huge relief as there has been trouble before getting film into Argentina, and we have a big packet for Cindy.

My first, rather tired, impression of B.A. was disappointing. I found it dirty, dilapidated and rather unattractive. I think this was partly bad luck as we were travelling through the less attractive and poverty-stricken areas of the city. The houses are French/Spanish in style where they are old, or very modern, all glass and angles. B.A. is built in a ''grid'' pattern like New York, all the streets run straight east-west, north-south. The main thoroughfares are wide and fast (there appears to be no speed limit) but the side streets are narrow and many of them are one-way only. The hotel Cindy recommended is in the older part of the town, quiet, just off the ''Florida'', a shopping area where there's even a Harrods, and where no cars are allowed. It

*Ticket is his labrador.

was hot and humid, and we were both tired, so we had a little sleep before wandering down to the Sheraton Hotel (about twenty minutes walk) and doing a bit of window shopping. Lots of lovely things, mostly very expensive, but virtually nothing unique to the Argentine except some rather awful woolly llamas. Lovely clothes, lovely bags, shoes, etc, but I would imagine all imported.

We found a really beautiful church, very ornate Spanish style with a magnificent reredos behind the altar, going up in steps to a huge monstrance at the top. Unfortunately mass was at 7.30 and we had to meet the Joys at six, so we were only able to go in for a moment. The Joys are charming, she's Spanish, tiny, rather shy and very helpful. The Argentines all talk so fast I can't understand them, but they can sometimes understand what I want, which produces another spate of Spanish.

22nd February

THIS a.m. after the usual telephone calls we went shopping, as Daddy had forgotten to pack his flannels. First we wrote postcards to all, so I hope you all got them; and armed with the phrase "please may I have some flannel trousers" off we went.

The next half-hour was hysterical. My carefully rehearsed phrase was so well understood that it produced a torrent of Spanish, which I thought meant they hadn't any flannel trousers. By now realizing I was a half-witted foreigner, the gentleman spoke more slowly to explain that flannel trousers were not available until the end of March or beginning of April! Faced now with asking for some other sort of trousers, I had to point to first one and then another pile. "Ah, poplin". Yes, they could do that for the senor.

The first pair fitted, but had buttons, not a zip. More gesticulations. The second pair, miraculously with a zip, were too small. I quite failed to make the salesman understand that the trousers were too tight (and also too short in the crutch) until I hit on the idea of reading the size of the pair that was too tight! Luckily I know the Spanish for 40. All was well. Daddy now had a navy blue pair of poplin trousers.

Now he wanted a grey pair. No grey 40. So off I set once more round the piles of trousers and finally I found a grey pair size 40. "Ah, alpacca". Well it could have been serge for all I knew. So we got a pair—buttons again. Finally a size 40 with a zip was produced. Now Daddy decided he needed a belt. That was downstairs, so after a very complicated financial transaction (19,000 pesos to the £1 leaves my brain reeling when buying things for 450,000 pesos), we tried to buy a belt. Apparently Argentinians don't wear belts. However, eventually we found one, which should have had a diamond buckle at that price. We tried to buy some dark shirts, but again size was the problem, so after a few false starts we gave up.

We were bidden to the British Embassy for lunch at 2 p.m., and I must say driving through the town north-west I changed my dismal view of B.A. That part is much prettier, cleaner with wider streets, and some lovely old houses with wrought-iron balconies and some arched windows. The Embassy is attractive, large and with a lovely garden with some beautiful trees.

The Ambassador and his wife were charming, but I always get an inferiority complex with diplomats, they always seem to know where every place in the world is (and expect you to as well) and they are great lovers of art, painting, opera, gardens and everything I am bad at. However, I think it went off well.

We then rushed off with Mrs Joy to buy a huge cheese for Mavis Hunt* in Port Stanley. It was suggested we took melons as well, but Daddy vetoed this as we are already heavily laden and are somewhat alarmed to hear that LADE, the Argentine airline we fly with to Stanley, are tiresome over how much luggage you have. I can't think what we'll do if they won't take it all, as we're not coming back here on the way back.

This evening Daddy is having a private meeting with Senor Costa Mendez, rather important, he's the Foreign Minister. And then the Joys are coming in for a drink about nine. No-one eats here until nine or ten or even later, but as we have to be up at 5.30 to catch our plane I hope we shan't be too late. It has been lovely here today, sunny, but cooler and not so humid. I would have loved to have gone out into the country, which I believe is lovely, but we haven't time with only one plane a week to Stanley. I can't believe it's all really happening and we'll be in Stanley tomorrow. It seems a very, very long way from London.

23rd February

WE LEFT the hotel at 7 a.m., I personally feeling rather bleary-eyed. On arrival at the domestic flights airport, there was no-

*Wife of H.E. Sir Rex Hunt, the Governor of the Falklands.

one at the LADE desk. As time went on I became convinced that the flight had been cancelled, which I was told quite cheerfully by our courier Daniel did happen sometimes. However, all was well and we eventually boarded the plane (all one class, a Fokker Friendship I think and rather cramped).

LADE is an Air Force airline run and staffed by Air Force crews. The pilots were first class, but the stewardesses! Gone were the smiles of welcome. Grim-faced stewardesses allotted you your seat, one wouldn't have dreamt of asking to go and sit by a window or further back. Never once during the whole flight, which took from 8.30 a.m. to 3.30 p.m., including five stops, did I see either of them smile except at the pilots.

It was the sort of flight I loathe, shortish "hops", calling at four places in Argentina and eventually Commodoro Rivadavia. The country seemed barren, desert-like and dull. Commodoro has to be seen to be believed. It's an oil town; the surrounding country is completely barren, grim rock-strewn hills come right down to the sea, the only greenery being trees and shrubs planted by the local inhabitants in their gardens. I have seldom seen such a depressing place in my life. It resembles the coal-mining towns of the 1930's in grimness, but of course is relieved by the sun, the sea and a reasonably unpolluted beach (so I'm told).

Although we flew on from Commodoro to Stanley in the same plane, all our luggage had to be unloaded and go through customs again, and then be reloaded, the first instance of military irritation we had encountered. Then when we came to board, two very attractive but grim-faced air force policewomen searched all our hand luggage, passports included. As the passport investigator could not speak or read English she must have found a lot to interest her, leafing through the pages, very slowly. It is really quite ridiculous. Presumably, it's the Argentine Government's way of retaliating over the Falklands wishing to be British. They have also cut the number of flights from Argentina to Stanley to one a week instead of two, all rather childish.

We arrived here in Stanley to find it very windy but sunny and quite warm. Rex Hunt, the Governor, was there to meet us with the famous maroon London taxi, complete with Governor's flag. We felt very grand being driven back to Government House. To those who haven't been here G.H. resembles a rather superior Scottish stalking lodge, but very comfortable inside, nice furniture, comfy beds and some quite pretty curtains in the bedrooms.

We were given a cup of tea, two hours rest and then quite a large cocktail party. Daddy was fine, as having been here before he knew lots of people, but I found it all rather confusing and tried frightfully hard to remember names and who was whose wife or husband. The strain must have addled my brain even further as I heard myself, to my horror, expressing a wish to fly up to Darwin tomorrow to attend a local gymkhana. Knowing my love of flying in small planes, you will undoubtedly assume I've gone mad (probably) or was drunk (one glass of sherry), so I can only assume it was tiredness.

So there I was committed to flying up to Darwin in the morning. I even tried to unscramble it by remembering it was Ash Wednesday and we ought to go to Mass. Alas, Mass is at nine, plenty of time, so by now rather alarmed I abandon myself to my fate, and eventually totter to bed at 11 p.m.

24th February

TO MY relief it's fine and sunny, though windy. We went to Mass at nine, rather a charming church. Robin Pitaluga, with whom I'm going to Darwin, rang to say "10.30 off," so off we went. To my surprise, and relief, I really enjoyed the flight. He has a little four-seater Cessna. The wind was so strong we had to fly at 2,500—3,000 feet, it was too rough lower than that. As there was a head wind it took us fifty minutes instead of thirty, but at least I saw some of East Falkland. It does remind me of Scotland, but no trees, much larger flat surfaces, a very indented coastline and lowish hills (nothing over 2,000 feet) with a lot of smaller ridges covered in what looked like scree or shale.

The gymkhana when it started was hilarious. It was the annual "holiday break" for the Falkland Island Company farms. The company are by far the biggest landowners in the Falklands and Darwin is where the manager, Brooke Hardcastle, lives. The actual gymkhana took place on Goose Green settlement, some two miles from Brooke's house. There were races, both mounted and on foot, as well as the usual bending races, potato races and musical chairs. There being no chairs, which anyway would have blown away in the wind, you had to claim a peg driven into the ground when a whistle blew. There were several events which were new to me, including a one-mile trotting race. The horses, mostly ponies, are all regularly used for shepherding and the riders were all shepherds.

The children's gymkhana is on Friday. There were only about twenty riders, and usually male and female were not in the same race, except for Gretna Green and threading the needle.

No one wore hats, or riding clothes, and the horses all wore their usual working "gear", as they call tack. This is rather difficult to describe. Basically the bridle is in two parts, first a kind of rawhide head collar with no fastening, loose enough to slip on and off, with one long rein for tying up (all rawhide, they make their own tack). Over this is a single strap over the head with a very long-cheeked curved bit, leather thong curb and one rein and a brow-band. The reins are held in one hand, never two, and you neck-rein always. Although the bits seem severe, you hardly have to touch the horse's mouth and I didn't see one horse with a sore mouth, ill-fitting "gear" or apparently uncomfortable.

The saddles are weird. First a blanket, then a sort of western-type saddle with a high back and front, usually made of wood (the back and front, not the bit you sit on). Over this a highly complicated rawhide cinch or girth. No buckles but a double ring, with the cinch wound round and round in a most intricate fashion. Then, over all this, a huge sheepskin held on by another type of circingle. It all looked very complicated but was obviously extremely comfortable to ride on for hours on end, as they do. The stirrups are western broad leather base, and held together by a thong under the horse's belly. This apparently helps if the horse bucks, which they do frequently, though I never saw one misbehave today. They also ride with something like two leather sausages (big) tied to the front of the saddle, and again joined by a thong underneath like a kind of huge elongated roll. They weren't using them today, but they always do when riding young newly "tamed" horses, or with renowned bucking horses. The whole effect is curiously cumbersome, and there always seems to be some thong dangling down from somewhere, which gives the horses a very untidy appearance. None of the horses are shod. They never go on a road and there are no stony tracks.

They ride enormous distances, 35 miles in one day, riding one horse leading two others, either tied to each other by a neck-thong, both led on the right-hand side, or tied to the first (or second or third) horse's tail, Indian style. I saw six led like this.

H.M.S. *Endurance* in pack ice between Graham Land and Adelaide Island, photographed from one of her helicopters. *Bob Mahoney*

A.B. on the deck of *Endurance* in fine weather. *Bob Mahoney*

The idea is you ride your horse for two hours, then put the gear on to horse No. 2 and then after another two hours, on to horse No. 3. It makes sense when you think about it.

I was very much impressed by the great enthusiasm of the riders, and by how much they enjoyed what we have come to regard as children's games. They entered into the spirit of the competitions and I never heard one complaint, nor a sour remark or "it's not fair" type of comment. During the trotting race if you broke into a canter you had to circle; everyone circled when they had to without being told; in fact though there was terrific competition for a £1 first prize, there was absolutely no cheating. I wonder if the children are so fair-minded and sporting, I wish I could see them. If they are they could give our own gymkhana children something to think about.

The ponies themselves are all Island bred and very much cross-breeds. Welsh cob is evident in one or two, also Argentine polo pony, Highland, a bit of Arab and one quarter Shetland. Quite how the half Shetland mum got here I can't think. The great problem is to overcome the interbreeding. If a stallion (or mare) tends to produce a certain weakness it's very hard to eradicate it with so much interbreeding, though they do import new blood at fairly regular intervals from Argentina.

At lunch I was invited to go to the manager's house and we had a large party and a very good lunch. Brooke Hardcastle's son is married to a girl from Buntingford, Hertfordshire, he met her when he was at agricultural college in England. She's a charming girl and seems blissfully happy. He is equally a charming young man, assistant manager on a farm called North Arm, which rather surprisingly appears to be at the southern end of East Falkland.

After lunch there were more races, and we left before the finish, I am glad to say, as I was really very tired by then having stood out all day in a warm but very strong wind. There is one absolutely extraordinary "time" here (or rather two), one is "Stanley or local" time, three hours behind England, and one is "camp" time, one hour later (four hours behind England). So on a half-hour flight from Stanley to Darwin leaving Stanley at 10.30 a.m. you arrive in Darwin at 10 a.m., all rather confusing to a tourist. I had said we'd be back at 5.30 and suddenly realised it would in fact be 6.30 Stanley time, so some hurried radio calls were made to G.H. Our flight back was much more bumpy, but with such a strong tail-wind only took twenty minutes, so everyone was in a muddle and Daddy was just about to get into a bath at G.H., having had a busy day, when they rang to say I was due in at the airport at any moment.

Apart from his various meetings Daddy seems to have bought himself some very smart clothes for *Endurance*, he will look rather like a cross between a retired admiral and a harbour-master with his navy yachting-type cap, navy trousers, navy slop-shirt and some rather startling blue and bright yellow running shoes. Still, as long as he is comfortable and warm enough, who cares.

We were hustled out for a drink when I got back, I only just had time to change. After supper I was longing to go to bed. I could hardly keep my eyes open, but Daddy and Rex went off to play snooker so I felt I had to talk to Mavis, eventually tottering upstairs at 11.30 p.m. I can't think how the Hunts manage to stay up so late and yet be up bright and early, it would kill me. H.M.S. *Endurance* arrives tomorrow, and I gather we sail tomorrow night. I am somewhat alarmed by Mavis saying I should take at least one long dress (I've only got one, not suitable for climbing up a companion way) and should wear a dress every night for dinner! I can hardly believe it. I've brought skirts, so they'll have to do. I have one short dress but I can't wear it every night and it doesn't wash. I am feeling somewhat alarmed by the prospect of four weeks on *Endurance.* I am terrified of saying or doing something wrong. If it wasn't that I'm longing to see Cindy I think I'd turn tail and run. It all sounds alarming and very much a man's world.

Endurance

25th February

ENDURANCE is in harbour! Nick Barker, her Captain, is arriving here at 11.30 a.m. I don't know yet when we embark.

We had a very nice lunch with Nick Barker at G.H. He brought with him a Commander Ponsonby who is in charge of an M.O.D. camera crew (civilian) who are making a film of *Endurance* in the Antarctic. Believe it or not he is the son of Gilbert Ponsonby, Daddy's late cousin. Really, what a family!

We had a hectic last-minute shopping spree. I tried to get some of the special stamps being printed for the Princess of Wales' birthday which are not available at home. I stupidly asked for all the first day cover stamps and couldn't imagine why it took the good lady nearly half an hour to produce them. To my amazement about twenty different stamps were handed over. They are really rather charming, but of course they weren't what I wanted; there were no Princess of Wales ones. However, I duly sent them off to Sarah* at vast expense, as I feel they may be quite valuable one day. Some of them are really lovely stamps.

We finally came on board H.M.S. *Endurance* at 4 p.m. The amount of stuff we had was unbelievable. We have a very nice cabin about the size of a couchette with two bunks one above the other, a wardrobe and some drawers. (What a lot of room sea-boots take up). We also have a day cabin with desk, chairs and a somewhat hard sofa, and a BAR. When we arrived the day cabin was literally stuffed full with our luggage, you couldn't move at all, so I pushed Papa out and unpacked my stuff, and then his, and the suitcases went into store. The M.O. was detailed to look after us and so was the Captain's steward, both charming. A life of luxury indeed; rather nice to be peaceful after rushing about since we arrived on Sunday. We had dinner with the Captain, and drinks beforehand in the wardroom, where we met the other officers. We had begun our voyage by then and I found the movement of the ship difficult; I seem to

*A grand daughter.

fall all over the place. No sea legs. The ship's officers are charming, and look very smart in white shirts, black trousers and scarlet cummerbunds for evening wear.

We went to bed early. I have the top bunk as I thought Papa would never get up there. It's quite a haul, and worse getting down.

26th February

AMAZINGLY we both slept quite well in spite of the motion. God bless Stugeron, though it makes me feel rather stupid. This a.m. we went to the hydrographics rooms, where I tried to take in the various projects they are hoping to carry out. It was all very interesting, if very much above my head. We are, I believe, going on a tour of the ship later this morning.

* * * * *

We have now had our tour of the ship, two hours of it. Interesting though it was, I must say I found it rather long, though the Hydrographic Department was fascinating, and Daddy was very excited about the telegraph/teleprint and radio room, which seemed quite incomprehensible to me. I think Vicky, Mops and Cindy would have been fascinated, also Tim. We also visited the met room which Papa seemed to understand rather well, needless to say I could not. The helicopter hangars were impressive, though the fact that the choppers are 26 years old fills me with alarm.

Am now sitting in our cabin, Papa is feeling a bit queasy and has gone up to the bridge. The swell is ''moderate'' but there's quite a lot of movement, difficult to walk about in. I must say looking at a ''calm'' sea with moderate swell, I simply cannot imagine how Mops* could possibly have managed to cope with it all in such a tiny boat. I have always been amazed and enormously proud of her yachting achievements, but I don't think I ever really appreciated one iota of the cold, wet and discomfort that goes into ocean racing, quite apart from the seasickness. Even with Stugeron, I wish the ship wouldn't wiggle so; my hand-writing is not improved by the sudden lurch she gives every now and then over and above the normal pitching and plunging.

*Mops, Maria's eldest daughter, who had just sailed her own boat across the Atlantic.

Quite apart from the fact that this is an epic journey for us, it may well be an epic journey for everyone, if this really is the last voyage *Endurance* will ever make except for going home. I have tried to take in as much as I can of the very involved situation regarding the goings-on between Argentina and Britain, but Daddy really has the picture much more clearly. There is more to this journey, and every other one *Endurance* has made, than I ever imagined. There's also some rather interesting, if alarming, bits of information regarding the other country's activities, but very confidential.

We are apparently in Drake's Passage and have two more days sailing before the "fun" starts at Marguerite Bay on the Graham Land Peninsula in the Antarctic. The "fun" I gather is a hectic time rushing about in choppers delivering mail and stores, transporting equipment, etc., but more on that when it happens. Off to have a drink now with the Captain.

27th February

WAS woken this morning at 5 a.m. by the crash of bottles, to discover we were in decidedly rougher waters than before. Before long tables were overturning, chairs skidding about, and even staying in your bunk required some concentration. Apparently we are now in Drake's Passage, agreed to be the most notoriously unreliable bit of ocean in the world. We're lucky to have comparatively calm conditions.

The captain's tour, to which Daddy and I were not looking forward, turned out to be hilarious. *Endurance* has no stabilisers, so we are rolling in the swell; and boy, are we rolling. Everyone grabs anything they can and holds on tight. Chairs scoot across the cabin, and everything possible is stowed away. The Captain emerged from his cabin, whistles blew, we were all awaiting the start of the tour, when the ship gave a tremendous roll. Daddy lost his balance, put his hand out to save himself and managed to knock the guard off the fire extinguisher, and his hand landed on the button. Foam flew out in a terrific gush like an oil strike, straight on my feet. I jumped back into our cabin and was, to my shame, convulsed with laughter. For one frozen second no-one moved, and foam gushed out with increasing strength. I have never laughed so much. Poor Daddy was marvellous, and everyone else remained poker-faced as a marine rushed forward with a small mop to try and mop up gallons of foam, which by now was happily sloshing up and down the corridor.

After that we inspected the ship, quite an ordeal in this weather. One really had to cling to something all the time. On entering a particular room, you either flew in rather uncontrollably if the "roll" was in the right direction, or were held, bent at an angle against the roll, before being jet-propelled inside as the "roll" started coming the other way. All in all an interesting experience I doubt I shall ever repeat. At the end whistles blew, congratulations given, beer given to especially hard-working areas, etc., etc. Just then the ship gave an unexpectedly vicious roll, everyone flew forwards, some through open cabin doors, some towards the stairways, some to cling to whatever they could find. It may not sound funny written down, but it really was.

The weather is worsening slightly. The chief steward, Deacon, who looks after the Captain and us, has just cheerfully announced "I shouldn't count on any lunch, sir, the galley is in a shambles". I know where the tuck shop is, so if I'm starving I shall lurch down there and buy some chocolate.

Stugeron is fine. I could never have stood this rolling without it. So far I've fallen out of a chair, and nearly squashed the Doctor who is so thin he wouldn't have stood a chance of "fielding" me, anyhow he was hanging on to a pipe or rail or something himself.

The weather worsened quite considerably, so this is written two days later as it has been impossible to write with all the rolling.

In spite of the "shambles" in the galley, lunch was produced which we ate on our knees in chairs firmly wedged, mine in a doorway. We tried to have a few people in for drinks that evening; most of the drink was consumed but a few glasses went hurtling through the air. Daddy had a nasty fall when the chair he was sitting in shot across the cabin and he fell half on my lap, half on the floor, banging his shoulder very hard on the floor and the sofa arm. His g. and t. landed in Francis Ponsonby's lap.

28th February

A VERY rough night, no-one got much sleep, it was all we could do to stay in our bunks and the sailors slept on the floor, I gather. About 5 a.m. Daddy nobly struggled up (he's in the bottom bunk) to wedge once again the "bottle" drawer which was weaving its way across the cabin accompanied by ominous clonks and crashes. By ten the sea had calmed down and we were able to hold a short church service in the seamen's dining hall. Three rousing hymns (unaccompanied), Daddy read the lesson, a prayer for calm weather and the seaman's prayer. Very simple but very charming, about twenty of us all told.

After church we went to the wardroom (officers' mess) and watched the film *More British than the British* which Anglia made about the Falklands. It really is very good, the Islanders really do feel very strongly about being British but whether any long-term peaceable solution can be evolved I don't know. Like so many things, it's just been mishandled in the past, and shelved or dealt with rather feebly since George Brown, then Foreign Secretary, "gave away" the Falklands. At least, he is reputed to have said "Falkland Islands—give them away, give away Gibraltar too" when asked once again about the problem. I don't feel competent to go into all the whys and wherefores, but the more I hear the more alarmed I feel by the lack of understanding and the wishy-washy excuses being dealt out by the various Ministries.

We had a fairly quiet afternoon, everyone was exhausted after a sleepless night. It's drizzling and there's nothing to see on deck beyond the odd wandering albatross or petrels. Daddy went to sleep and I knitted, rather like home. The deck is too slippery and the roll too great to walk anywhere, so we've had a quiet day. Rather nice really.

1st March

DADDY woke at six to report icebergs and rushed up to the bridge. It has now got very cold, we are inside the Antarctic Circle, about 62° 32′ south.

Daddy has bought himself a very smart navy blue naval officer's jersey with elbow and shoulder patches and epaulettes. Nick suggested I embroider a House of Lords "badge" on the epaulettes. The land, Graham Land, the most northerly point in the peninsula, is really magnificent. The sea has calmed down completely, huge icebergs are around everywhere, and the land mass reminds me of the Alps, big rocky snow-covered mountains (actually I don't think they are very high). The icebergs are beautiful, and some have almost cobalt blue streaks to them where there are fissures and light penetrates. Most have a bluish-green tinge, especially just above and below the water line. We had breakfast on a table today, not on our laps, marvellous. Then helicopter drill in the hangar at 8.30. I am rather alarmed by the prospect of my first chopper flight, these Wasps are strictly operational, no comforts and no doors either, so we're going to be jolly cold. Thank God for Mop's thermal underwear, sea-boots, balaclavas and gloves. We're going to need them. We've already had a couple of snow showers and the wind from the South is bitter. I got a Telex from Cindy saying they were longing to see us, but I don't think we get there for another ten or fourteen days as we visit other bases, put hydrographers ashore, and of course the camera crew, who are I think as worried about their equipment going in a Wasp as I am about myself.

1st March p.m.

NEVER have I had such a wonderfully exciting day.

After lunch we were all togged up in the most incredible gear, known as goon suits. Orange rubber with welded seams, no shape except for two arms and two legs with feet rather like a rubber baby-grow and just about as difficult to put on, as it goes over your parka (fur-lined jacket), sea boots, etc., and a draw-string pulls it tight around your neck. Over this you wear a U-shaped life-jacket, hard like a horse's collar, with straps between your legs. As one can by now barely move, one's progress to the chopper for the beginner must have looked as funny as it felt. As all the goon suits are made to fit men up to 6 feet 4 inches (you tie them at the knee to avoid falling on your nose) you can imagine what I looked like. Even the chopper pilots were convulsed with laughter and the photographers had a field day. Rather annoyingly for me Daddy looked perfectly at home, if rather bewildered. Add to this a pair of metal ear-muffs to deaden the sound and the mind really boggles at the picture I made.

Getting into the chopper was equally hilarious. There are no doors and only two seats, one for the pilot and one other which I had. It's about three feet from the ground, and you all know how agile I am. Once in, I was strapped in, and poor Daddy and Nick were rather unceremoniously dumped on the floor

One of the choppers filming *Endurance* sitting on a large ice-floe.

''en face'' of me. The navigator nonchalantly sat on the edge opposite me, one leg dangling, trying to stifle his laughter. I have never enjoyed a flight so much, it was breathtaking.

So was the scenery, snow-covered mountains, superb icebergs, pack ice in the sea below us. A few minutes later and we were put down so smoothly on the snowy shores by the B.A.S. station of Rothera, in Marguerite Bay, the furthest south we'll get, 1,000 miles from the South Pole itself, and about 1,000 miles south of the Falkland Islands. The photographers, blast them, had got there first and had a field day snapping us tumbling out of the chopper and trying to walk over the shore in our goon suits. I trust it was not filmed. We then proceeded to try and get out of life-jackets and goon suits with, I gather, side-splitting results, which again were photographed. I'll have to try and get the negatives and destroy them as ''undignified''.

We were then introduced to the Station Commander and three enchanting nine-week-old Husky pups. The film men wanted the pups to run towards the camera, so we tried to hold them like greyhounds in the traps and on the word ''go'', let them go. Of course they all went in different directions, amid much laughter and cries of ''retake''. I then went and joined Daddy and Nick for a tour of the base.

It's really two large huts, heated, with running water, but chemical loos, as any sewage would freeze long before it got to the sea. They have a super dining hall, lounge and small but quite well-stocked library, and bedrooms (four bunkbeds to a room), sick back and surgery. The other hut contains the work-room, repair shops, carpenter's shop and two kennels for whelping bitches. We were lucky enough to see four two-week-old pups all fast asleep looking like part-coloured labrador pups with quite short coats. After our tour we went outside and saw the ''lines'' where the Husky dogs live. Each dog is staked down on a chain to a sort of iron ring set in a long steel ''rope''. The chain is long enough for them to move about, but not long enough for them to reach each other or they fight. When they are being harnessed to the sledges you have to be very careful to make them sit until they are harnessed, then ''go''. Sometimes they go, sometimes they turn on each other and a massive dog-fight ensues, not very funny.

All too soon we dressed up again and flew back. It really had been the most fantastic day, much more exciting than I've made it sound. There was a celebration in the wardroom tonight as one of the officers had been promoted today. We all had a drink and wished him luck.

We got under way again very quickly, going north to Faraday B.A.S. camp and Brabant Island. We then visit another base (Argentinian, I think) and possibly Palmer Base (U.S.A.) before returning to Faraday and eventually to Rothera. At the moment there are magnificent icebergs all around us, one or two quite near, and as we have the doctor and the secretary on watch, the captain, Nick, with whom we feed, has to keep leaping up to check our progress among the ''bergs''.

Icebergs really are fascinating things, white greeny-blue or even cobalt blue, some with long arms spreading out beneath the water-line. Only a sixth of any iceberg shows above the water, sometimes even less if there are arms or ledges spread out beneath the surface. This has been the most fascinating trip I have made, or am likely to make. I just wish you could all be here to enjoy it and marvel at the incredible grandeur of it all.

The other thing that has struck me very forceably is how terribly friendly every one of the crew is, from Nick downwards; they go out of their way to be kind and helpful, and are always ready to give advice, or information, and are particularly helpful to me, which is nice of them. I think that most of them knowing Cindy and Annie—known, I gather, throughout the ship's company as "C and A"—has helped me as "C and A" are wildly popular. One rather amusing thing; apparently when I went round the ship on the captain's tour on our first day there was great consternation about my reaction to the type of female art displayed in the cabins. I regret to say I never noticed it, but haven't let on.

I think by a sudden bumping, we must have run over a very small iceberg. The sea is getting up a bit, so it's not easy to write. We are steaming north, leaving Adelaide Island to starboard. It looks a very dreary, bleak and barren land in the failing light. There's no vegetation down here at all, so of course no animals, except seals, which live on fish. It's an unbelievably beautiful place when the sun shines, with mountains, inlets and bays dotted with icebergs of every size. But when the

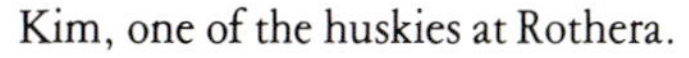

Kim, one of the huskies at Rothera.

Icebergs really are fascinating things . . . only a sixth of any iceberg shows above the water.

sun goes in the skies turn grey, and it snows and blows. You can imagine the rigours and terrible conditions Scott and Amundsen encountered here, with no warm *Endurance* to return to each evening.

2nd March

FOR some reason we both overslept, perhaps the result of flying, fresh air, and general excitement yesterday. I wrote some letters and got some special stamps which are printed for B.A.S. which the Falkland Island Post Master General, who is on board, is going to stamp for me at Faraday Base. Just before lunch we began to see really superb "bergs" as we nosed our way in towards Faraday. This is a B.A.S. station dealing with the ionosphere and the ozone layer, which means precisely nothing to me; but it seems to be a rather specialised met. department dealing also in radio. After lunch we dressed up in Mop's and Johnnie's invaluable warm clothing and went by boat to

Faraday, as sadly there was no sun and too low a cloud base for flying. The choppers should be working flat out tomorrow dropping supplies on Brabant Island.

I do not find Faraday so interesting as Rothera. It's not nearly such an attractive place, being on a small island, and the work done here is so technical it's really difficult to appreciate its importance. The men are charming, they live and work in and around the base (two huts). There's no field work, which must be pretty awful, especially in the long antarctic winter.

We came back after about an hour and watched the boats bringing back the photographers and two rather drunk sailors who'd gone ashore. They were dealt with! Then we stayed up on deck watching the icebergs slide by as we made for the open sea and headed north again to Brabant Island. I suddenly remembered it was Eleanor's tenth birthday tomorrow, so I sent off a cable on Marisat (Satellite telephone). I do hope she gets it in time and that it has either *Endurance* or Antarctica on it. I suppose it's too much to hope it might have penguins and seals round the edge.

The sea's getting up again, I'm afraid we're in for a rough night.

3rd March

WELL, we got our rough night. Daddy has become totally involved in shiplife and rushed up to the bridge during the night when there was a horrendous crash, so what with him leaping about, and the drawers, chairs and tables doing their usual rough weather cavorting, not much sleep was had by either of us. In fact the weather had been so bad during the night that one of the fuel drums due to be dumped on Brabant Island today was cut in half by the steel hawser lashing it, and five others were dented and started leaking fuel, most of which was all over the forward upper deck.

Sadly we have more drizzle and mist, and the choppers can't fly, so we're having to bypass one of two dumping places at Brabant Island and try round the eastern side, hoping to get better weather in the lee of the island and the mainland. We went up on deck briefly to see a really huge iceberg at least sixty metres out of the water (so about 300 metres below), quite a berg. There is a plan afoot to tow bergs of this size from round here (or as near to their destination as you can find them) to countries chronically and habitually short of water like Saudi Arabia. Apparently it's feasible, the bergs don't melt much and are so huge the amount of berg eventually arriving at Saudi Arabia or wherever would still be of immense value. It all sounds rather odd, but I am told it really could be done.

The stores we are hoping to drop on Brabant Island are for some expedition or project for next autumn, I believe. If there is no longer either *Endurance* or a replacement, which seems in doubt, B.A.S. will have great difficulty keeping its bases supplied. For instance, *Endurance* brought and collected mail from Faraday, the first mail they had had since Christmas as the B.A.S. ships haven't been back to Stanley since December. I can't go into the whys and wherefores of keeping a naval ship in these waters, but the more I see the more I am quite certain that John Nott has no idea what they are going to lose in prestige, help to the stations, and very valuable information on many subjects which a naval vessel alone can supply. I only wish some big-wig could come out here and see for himself, and really put the case properly.

Very dismal news from Washington re the Falklands; deadlock, the Argentinians are threatening "sanctions" against the Islands, which they refer to as the "Malvinas". I suppose that means they'll cut the once-weekly flights to Commodoro and B.A. to once a fortnight, or even cut them altogether, and refuse medical help over serious cases which the little hospital at Stanley simply is not equipped to deal with. The Chileans would love to help, but can't as they would have to fly from Punta Arenas over Argentine airspace. It really is very sad, and it has been so desperately badly mishandled in the past that I can see very little hope of a peaceful settlement. Nick insists we must be firmer, but I very much doubt we shall be. Our foreign policy seems to be appeasement, not firmness.

We are now entering some straights, hopefully to get in to Brabant Island on the east side. It's pouring with rain but calmer. The flight commander brought us some krill he found on the deck this morning, and the met officer has photographed them for us, and has promised to get us a bottle and some formalin to keep them in. They are quite small, sandy coloured with faint pink stripes and huge black eyes, very like our own shrimps. I gather ther are two sorts, one larger and much pinker, but I think they may lose their colour when they are out of the water and die.

The weather eventually improved sufficiently for the choppers to fly briefly. They took some men on to Brabant to find a suitable place to dump the stores for Chris Furze and his party. Unfortunately once on the island they couldn't find any place safe enough to leave the stores. The island is very mountainous and has many glaciers which tend to break off vast bits and cover the shore, and the snow had so many crevasses that no suitable place could be found. So, if he does come in September, Chris Furze will simply have to bring his equipment with him.

Going into Paradise Bay to Almirante Brown station (Argentinian) we saw a really wonderful sight. The channel is fairly narrow with huge mountains up to 8,000 feet further inland. The Bay is actually part of the peninsula of Graham Land; huge icebergs, luckily mostly near the shore, and wonderful glacial formations with huge caves at the water line. We saw two whales, don't know what sort, and quite a lot of penguins. There's an apparently "summer only" Chilean base at the entrance to Paradise Bay, where there were huge flocks of penguins. It looked rather amusing with orange-painted huts, and penguins strutting about as if they were the scientists busy

Going into Paradise Bay to Almirante Brown station we saw a really wonderful sight.

The Argentinian base of Almirante Brown (seen from *Endurance*)

about their work. Sadly the visibility wasn't very good, but even then Paradise gave one an idea of how beautiful it would be if the sun shone. Apparently it's very rare for it to rain here at this time of the year, but one of the Faraday chaps told me that they had had a lot of rain this summer, much more than usual.

We anchored just off the camp of Almirante Brown. Daddy and I were on the bridge. I hope we weren't in the way, they are all so charming to us and they even try and explain things to me. It was dramatic nosing our way in, 300 metres, 280 metres, shelving slowly, depth soundings every minute or so. Also "so many cables" from shore. No fuss, no flurry, just all very calm and professional. We dropped anchor but the water was too deep, and it started to drag, so we had to pull it up again, quite a slow job, and go further into another smaller bay where the water was shallower.

It must be really lovely in the sun with these high mountains and glaciers. We didn't go ashore, it was too late, but a small Argentinian boat with the camp commandant (a doctor) and a geophysicist came aboard. Neither spoke any English, the doctor looked for all the world like a Cuban guerilla in khaki shirt and trousers and knee-length laced leather boots. The

Being greeted at Rothera by the B.A.S. base commander. *Bob Mahoney*

Us with members of the B.A.S. staff at Rothera during our first visit there. *Bob Mahoney*

The whaler pulls away from *Endurance* for the visit to the Argentinian base at Almirante Brown. Conditions were anything but comfortable. *Bob Mahoney*

Below, the Antarctic can be really lovely when the sun shines, but it is also an awe-inspiring part of the world. *M.B.*

scientist, who told me he lived in B.A. and had four children, and had been here two months and would be here another ten, was a large jolly young man in a blue windcheater and grey trousers. I found the commandant rather difficult to talk to but we all tried hard over dinner, and we had Mario the Uruguayan to translate.

Mario Fontonot is a commander in the Uruguayan navy. I find Mario charming and he speaks marvellous English. He was taken on *Endurance* on a sort of friendly attachment. One night in the mess he told me all about his family. Mario is of Italian descent, as are so many Uruguayans and Argentinians. Galtieri himself is of Italian origin. Mario's family all talk Italian at home. He supports wholeheartedly the claim of Argentina to the Falklands, as far as I can see simply because of their geographic location. I tried to explain that the islanders themselves considered they were British, but I fear it fell on deaf ears.

It appears that the Argentinians have sent their summer scientists home, only eight are left, and they are shutting the camp down at the end of the year. They say their work here is finished, but we none of us believe that, though what the real reason is we cannot say; probably to lay claim to the territory as Argentinian as they have settled it. I am sure there's an underlying motive.

We were then invited down to the wardroom, where there were five more Argentinians, none of whom spoke English. But we managed to converse somehow with the help of beer, whisky, and general gesticulations and efforts on everyone's part to try some word in the other's language. The Argentinian cook got rather merry, and when they finally left at 11.30 he started kissing the English officers good-bye, to their intense embarrassment. I fled behind a door and firmly said "Adios, manana".

4th March

DURING the night it snowed hard, there's a fair old wind blowing and apparently two smallish (luckily) icebergs knocked into us during the night. I heard nothing, nor did Daddy. We were going ashore to visit the base at 8.30 but the visibility's too bad, so we've put that off for an hour or two. If the weather improves Daddy, Mario, I and some sailors will go ashore in the whaler for a short tour of the base, before setting sail for Palmer

Base (U.S.A.) further north. Apparently it's likely to be fairly rough again, which doesn't make writing easy, so I'm scribbling down impressions now.

They are sending the whaler in with a small party of Spanish-speaking men, including the doctor. Nick suggested that as he couldn't go (he felt he should stay in the ship as she was in a fairly hazardous anchorage) we shouldn't go either, as it was wet, cold, and snowing. However Daddy said he thought he should go, as it was important for him from a political point of view to have seen an Argentine base, even if it is one they are closing down. Nick agreed, but to my utter disappointment said he thought I shouldn't go.

I'm sure he was right, and I didn't feel I could protest, but I felt very sad. I went on deck and watched the boat leave. Having seen the rope ladder they had to climb down into the boat, I think perhaps Nick was right. I'm not sure of my prowess in clambering down a rope ladder into a heaving boat and I am permanently terrified of being either in the way or a nuisance. I'm damn lucky to be here, and everyone has gone out of their way to be kind, so I don't want to do anything to irritate them, but I would have loved to have gone. Actually there was a drama, a sailor cut the top of his finger off in one of the doors. The doctor was in the boat, so they had to recall it, disembark the doctor and start all over again. I thought Daddy looked rather cold and miserable in the boat. I hope the visit does prove useful to him.

*　　*　　*　　*　　*

The sun has now come out and it really is a fabulous sight. We are steaming round towards the camp to save the boat from having to make the longer journey back. I shall be interested to hear what Daddy has to report on this base.

Daddy's back now, not very impressed with the base, perhaps not surprising as it's being run down. We set sail immediately for the American base at Palmer Island. The course lay through the Numayer Straits which is quite magnificent with snow-covered mountains and glaciers on both sides. Both the choppers were flying with the photographers taking pictures of *Endurance* going through this magnificent scenery, amid the usual fantastic icebergs in every shape you can think of. After about an hour we seemed to have left the Straits and were talking on the radio to Palmer Station asking them to dinner, and they extended an invitation to tea and a tour of the base. Great enthusiasm among the sailors as there appears to be a girl, by the sound of her voice as she came on the radio from Palmer Base quite young too.

Quite by chance I looked over to port and there to my amazement was a ship. My remark "What's that ship?" brought the swiftest action on the bridge I've yet seen. Binoculars grabbed, choppers called up to go and investigate—was it the *Bransfield** or not (she was supposed to be going further south to Rothera). However she turned out to be the U.S. Coastguard vessel *Glacier*, which is really a U.S. naval survey and scientific ship, twice the size of *Endurance*, and with two choppers. Some coastguard.

We called them up, they hadn't seen us. They were about five miles away and were also making for Palmer Base, but don't expect to arrive before 08.00 tomorrow, so with any luck we'll see her then. We then listened in to a fascinating conversation between *Glacier* and Palmer Base; that was when we heard the girl operator. Hope she comes up to expectations, she'll probably make a dead set for Daddy, girls always do. "And 'a Lord', gee what next!"

We went over to Palmer Base by boat, quite a swell running, quite easy going down the gangway, but to my horror the other end at Palmer Base was just an iron ladder! With the boat rising and dropping about five feet the ladder was horribly difficult for me at my advanced age, but I managed to grab it and climb up, helping hands are always forthcoming at the top. The film unit was having a ball with us all coming up the ladder. The base commander, Garth Brown, was charming as were the other members of the base that we met. There were two girl scientists, neither of whom was likely to produce wolf-whistles, though charming to talk to. We were given tea and a conducted tour of the base.

The main interest is the study of Krill, why it's more plentiful at some times of the year, its food, etc., etc. It was in fact very interesting, if above my head. We hadn't much time to talk to the scientists, which was a pity. Daddy and I were then given two Palmer Base T-shirts and two emblems, presumably to sew on our anoraks. I think I'll look rather smart with Palmer Base

*R.R.S. *Bransfield*, one of the supply ships operated by the British Antarctic Survey.

Antarctica on my puffa, wandering about on the marsh at home in Norfolk.

Our return journey very nearly ended in an accident. Going down the iron ladder was quite easy for me (and everyone else) but the swell was running higher and when we got out of the lee of the Base to *Endurance* herself—wow, it was different! First the boat got under the companion way, then Nick jumped nimbly across. Like a fool I went next. I put my foot on the edge of the boat, Nick grabbed my hand and the cox'n said "jump". Whether I hesitated a fraction or he got it wrong I don't know, I think a bit of both. I jumped too late, fell on my left knee, and the boat came up on the next wave right *under* the companion way. You've never heard such a crash. Luckily Nick held on like grim death and I got to my feet feeling very small. I may say the news that I had tried to drown the captain was all over the ship in five minutes flat, which did nothing for my confidence.

The U.S. Coastguard cutter *Glacier* at Palmer Base, with *Endurance's* choppers bringing off the "stores" and Dudley Docker in the foreground, returning from delivering us to coffee on board the vessel.

Contrasts

5th March

THIS morning was utterly fascinating, if for me another rather alarming occasion. We were invited over to the U.S. Coastguard cutter *Glacier.* She is an icebreaker, some 8,000 tons, and has scientists aboard her, as well as choppers, "helos" in American. First we went down a rope ladder to the whaler. Thank God they put a sling round me, around my back, which helps me up if I slip, some poor unfortunate sailor hanging on to my 12½ stone with all his might. I managed that all right, but, oh dear, when we got to *Glacier* the ladder seemed to be miles long, (actually it was about twice as long as *Endurance's*). Nick had the kindness to bring the sling with him and I did manage the climb, though with no helping hand at the top and no rope I landed on my knee, not the most impressive way to land on an American vessel. Daddy managed much better.

All the officers in full dress were waiting to receive us, looking incredibly smart with three or four rows of medals each. Captain Coste was actually charming and we went to his cabin to have some coffee. In *Endurance* the top and next deck down have wooden handrails up the "stairs" and metal ones on the lower decks. On *Glacier* all are metal "stairs", all rather grubby. The captain's cabin was huge, the size of the bridge here, and his "bedroom" where we left our coats had a bed, not a bunk, and a full-sized bathroom. All very plush.

We sat and drank coffee and talked for about an hour. Captain Coste was completely puzzled as to why a peer and his wife were aboard a naval ship in the Antarctic. I got Nick to explain and kept out of the conversation as much as possible. The captain seems to resent scientists. He said that he found ornithologists the most difficult of all. They were always rushing on to the bridge, binoculars at the ready, and consequently getting in the way. Nick, Francis and I burst into fits of laughter and had to explain that Daddy was a dedicated ornithologist, never separated from his binoculars. Even Daddy had to smile. Nick then explained that we were in *Endurance*, courtesy of the Royal Navy, to see Cindy and Annie in South Georgia.

The Captain was shattered by the thought of us abandoning our daughter and friend to seven months' isolation in a hut 7 feet by 12 feet on an antarctic island. He explained that his two daughters helped their mother in the house, and his sons mowed the lawns and cut the hedges. He implied that had the sons offered to lay the table or the girls to mow the lawn it would not be at all "the thing". I dared not admit that another of my daughters had just sailed across the Atlantic in her own 32 foot boat, and that the youngest was a flying instructor, in the process of becoming the youngest female commercial pilot.

There are four female officers and seventeen "women ratings" in *Glacier*, as well as a very pretty girl scientist from Texas studying marine geology, which means taking samples of the sea bed for analysis "back home". Amazingly enough she knew where Jill and Jim Bowen* are working in Texas, but hadn't met them.

We had a short tour of the ship—*v.* short, just the bridge and the chopper hangars. For some reason I couldn't fathom, their choppers couldn't fly to take off the "stores" from Palmer station, the stores being specimens and things like that, to go back to America for further study. So our two super pilots were asked to do the job, which they did very efficiently, much impressing Captain Coste, who, slightly tactlessly I thought, informed his pilots he wished they operated as efficiently. Apparently he has "union" restrictions with his flying staff. They can fly so many hours, quite rightly, but if they start at 8.30, say, and fly for two hours and then another hour during the afternoon, by 4.30 they can't fly any more because they've been on call for eight hours. It must be frustrating, as the flight deck men literally refuse to bend the rules at all, even if they have actually only flown one hour during the day.

I did not get the impression that there was a relaxed atmosphere on the *Glacier*. The captain obviously found scientists a bore and had no interest in their work. But he did love being in Antarctica. Quite what he thought his mission was if he didn't have scientists aboard, or supply them, I don't know. He never went ashore to see Garth Brown at Palmer Base, which seemed strange. I can't imagine Nick not going ashore to visit a British base when he was taking off stores (and personnel), unless the weather was so bad that he felt he

*The Buxton's former vets at home.

shouldn't leave his ship, as happened yesterday morning at Almirante Brown; and then he sent a senior officer to represent him and had ten of them on board for supper. And the Argentine commander and second-in-command to dinner in his cabin. So it was quite an eye-opener for me to find that the spirit of *Endurance* is rather British and not to be found everywhere by any means. It must lie with the captain to have a happy contented ship, and it says much for Nick that his is manifestly a very happy ship.

Both ladders safely negotiated personally on the way home. The coxswain jokingly remarked "You need to go on a marine commando course" as I landed rather ungracefully in the whaler. It really is nice to be back in *Endurance*; it's funny, but it felt like coming home.

I went round all the food stores this morning. Huge refrigeration rooms, at different temperatures for different things, and an enormous deep freeze room. It was all very interesting; they make all their own bread, thirty loaves a bag, one bag of flour lasting two days. They bake every afternoon, quite an undertaking, though they have some special additive I'd never heard of which makes the dough "prove" in an hour, so it's not quite so tedious as making bread at home. They mix the flour, yeast extract, this additive and water all together, knead it into dough, put it into a tin, leave for an hour to prove and rise and then into the oven. Just like that; sounds easy, doesn't it!

We are now under way again, going to try the Le Maire Straits on our way south again to Rothera, where I think, all being well, we should arrive at 15.00. The Le Maire Straits were reported by R.R.S. *Bransfield* to be blocked by ice two days ago, so it will be interesting to see whether we can in fact get through. And possibly more interesting still to see what happens if we can't. I believe a chopper is going ahead to make a reconnaissance, so we shouldn't actually get stuck, unable to go forwards or to turn.

* * * * *

Our journey through the Le Maire Straits was quite unbelievable. Daddy and I spent the whole afternoon on the bridge. The cliffs dark and menacing, with huge glaciers riddled with deep crevasses which gave the impression they might fall off into the straits at any moment. The straits are quite narrow,

Endurance in Marguerite Bay, with the boats and chopper landing stores at Rothera.

Some of the bergs were large, but we were able to nose round and avoid them.

but there seemed to be only a little brash (loose very thin ice), and a few "bergs", so the chopper went off to see what it was like further on, and reported several big bergs, but he thought quite passable. So we went on.

The camera chap was in the chopper and must have got some of the most spectacular shots of his life. The channel is six miles long and varies in width, but never less than half a mile. Some of the bergs were large, but we were able to nose round and avoid them. We saw several whales unconcernedly going about their business, one party looked like mother and half-grown child. Seals were plentiful and rather resented a large red "thing" bearing down on their little flat ice floes and disturbing their afternoon sleep in the sun. They raised their heads and hissed at us, leaving to the last moment their return to the sea. They are charming creatures, I believe they were crab-eater seals.

Daddy has seen what he thought was a leopard seal, but no-one else has. We finally got through the Le Maire Straits to find unbelievably huge bergs lying at the southern end. Some were sufficiently light to be rising and falling with the swell. I've never seen bergs rise and fall and even roll, like a ship, it was most dramatic. Now we are in the open sea and the swell is "moderate", which means that things fall over and cabin drawers slide out, but you can stand up.

6th March

WE WOKE late to find ourselves in a sea of pack ice and bergs. The sun was shining and we both got dressed hurriedly and dashed up on deck. It really was so lovely, miles and miles of pack ice, ice floes, icebergs and the mountains of Graham Land on one side and Adelaide Island on the other. Seals were everywhere lying on the pack; most refused to move unless they were obviously going to get crushed. They all raised their heads and hissed at us, but quickly lay down again to snooze after the danger had passed.

I cannot describe to you the beauty and sense of isolation, it's like being on another planet, being in an area of ice as far as the eye can see. It really is a curious feeling and infinitely beautiful. *Endurance* can break through ice of I think one metre (perhaps less) and can nose aside small bergs which crunch down the side with streaks of red paint left on the berg. Nick is anxious to go down an uncharted, hitherto unexplored, passage between Adelaide Island and Graham Land, so we are weaving about in the pack and have now gone astern into calmer waters. There's quite a swell in the pack, so we hope to launch the choppers for a recce to see whether we can get down this very narrow passage, which appears on the map to have one or two small islands in the narrowest stretch. This won't worry us, but the amount of ice and its thickness will. I am listening now to the chopper reporting to the bridge that there's a line of "fast" ice, no breaks in it ahead, but so far no decision has been made. It really is exciting and very spectacular.

Alas, the stretch of "fast" ice is too thick for us to break through, so we'll have to go round the north side of Adelaide Island and down to Rothera that way. We were going to have the *Bransfield* and some Rothera chaps here for supper tonight but we shan't get there in time. We have now turned round and are going to the north before turning west, then south, then east into Marguerite Bay (I think). The pack ice has got much thicker as the sea is freezing over and we've had to nose our way round some of the larger bits and break through the smaller ones.

The film crew are furiously photographing both from the ship and from the chopper. It must be a fabulous sight; the red-painted ship amidst literally miles and miles of ice, icebergs, and 7,000 feet snow-topped mountains and ice-blue glaciers in the background, both south and north of us. They are a magnificent crew, they say that it's been the most fantastic scenery they have ever filmed and are enthusiastic about the whole project. (It is, I gather, a film describing *Endurance's* part in our Antarctic activities, and will be for the cinema as a supporting film. I must find out when and where it comes out as it should be fabulous. The stills photographers have been having a field day, and have so far produced one of Daddy dressed in his goon suit being hauled up the rope ladder in the sling, when it was too rough for me to go. Not perhaps a very flattering photograph, but it does give one a good idea of what he had to contend with that day.)

Bransfield is at Rothera and sails again tomorrow for Faraday and Signy. I'm not yet sure whether we shall actually meet or not. We're now in the open sea, rather dull and the usual rolling. It was quite odd to see the pack ice rising and falling with the swell, with a completely calm sea. The thin layer of ice which I believe is called grease or pancake ice seems to reduce the swell to a sort of "oily" swell of longer, smooth undulations, which really looks rather odd rolling away (or towards you). There were a lot of crab-eater seals lying on their floes again, bobbing along happily, asleep in the sun. One or two skuas came and hovered over the bows of the ship for quite two minutes, about ten feet above the sailors' heads. I don't think they had ever seen a ship before, and were rather intrigued; perhaps they merely wanted food.

7th March

WE'RE now anchored in Marguerite Bay. *Bransfield* is here too and we are flying over for lunch, going at eleven so that Daddy and Nick can have a talk with Dr R. M. Laws, Director of the British Antarctic Survey, and Sir Donald Logan, who is looking into the safety regulations on British bases, I presume on account of the two poor chaps killed here last year, when they went down a crevasse on a skidoo.

This was at Rothera where they have, as far as I can see, plenty of room to move about in comparative safety, and do a good deal of "field" work as opposed to oceanic field work from a boat. Some of the stations are situated where it's too dangerous to take skis out, or skidoos. At those stations all the work has to be done from a boat, except for skiing across the frozen sea

The downdraught from the helicopter rotors creates a curious pattern on the water as it hovers alongside *Endurance*.

during the winter, should you so wish, and even this has to be undertaken with great care, as a sudden snowstorm (and they blow up with no warning here) produces a "white-out" and you would never find your way back to base or even know where you were.

I can hardly believe we've now been in *Endurance* for ten days. It's a remarkable experience. In one way it seems like only two days ago, in another we seem to have been here for ever. It's like living on another planet, especially when sailing through pack ice. I only wish I could have heard from the family, but I've not heard anything so far except one telex from Kathryn* nine days ago.

We had a fabulous flight to R.R.S. *Bransfield*. It took ten minutes to get there, and at least another ten to get dressed in our goon suits and life-jackets, and this time I was given a flying helmet, so I could hear the inter-com.

I've almost mastered the art of getting into a goon suit, I'm coming on. We landed very comfortably on *Bransfield's* deck. I

*Lord Buxton's Secretary in London.

felt rather as if I'd landed from Mars and probably looked as if I had too, to be met by the captain and Dick Laws—the first time I kissed anyone whilst wearing a flying helmet, probably the first time he had, too!

We had a nice tour of the ship, she's very plush compared to ours, 7,000 tons I think, huge bridge, very sumptuous captain's quarters. They only have 35 crew but can carry up to 56 extras in the way of scientists, F.I.D.S.* as they call them. The crew all have their own cabins, rather superior ones, and a superb mess, and a "lounge" and bar. Then there's a complete deck set aside for scientists with lounge and rather more spartan cabins with four bunks in each. It was explained that as F.I.D.S. have to live in a community at the bases, it's better they should not have separate accommodation on board ship. I didn't quite follow this argument, but suppose there must be something in it. Then the officers' quarters and wardroom, again quite large, and on the top deck the captain's quarters and some more cabins.

The *Bransfield* isn't much longer than *Endurance*, but is much broader in the beam, so gives the impression of being very light and airy, but I found her a bit like a floating hotel. Captain Stewart was very gracious. He has given me a super plaque of *Bransfield.* What with that, and a picture of *Glacier*, a Palmer Station emblem, and a fantastic picture taken yesterday of *Endurance* going through the pack ice, we really are collecting a few souvenirs. After our tour we had lunch, which was good, if you like curry, which luckily I do. Then it was time to get into goon suits again and say goodbye.

Daddy and I flew first with Tony Ellerbeck, the flight commander, and hovered over some islands to see if there were Emperor penguins on them, but no luck. So we came back, going quite low, and saw lots of seals lying out on the ice quite unconcerned by the noise. We are now doing some "charting", which is where the ship sails up and down between two given points over a different route each time (in lines 250 metres apart) and then the hydrographers have huge fun putting squiggles on their charts which all look just the same to me, but are obviously intelligible to them, as they produce proper charts from their squiggles. All very necessary, but slightly boring, for very spoilt passengers, who can nevertheless get on with reading and writing, as the sea is like a millpond today.

*Falkland Islands Dependencies Scientists.

8th March

WOKE this a.m. with the first sign of a cold, very boring.

Tony Ellerbeck came to ask if we wanted to go into Rothera for a look round, but in fact quite apart from not feeling too good myself the weather was rather foul, misty with snow clouds, no sun. So we said no thank you. Daddy has a mass of papers to go through. He hasn't really had much time for reading and writing, we've been so well entertained.

The Antarctic Treaty and all that is rather above my head, but fascinating, though it's easy to fall into the trap of coming down here for a week or so and thinking you know all the answers, as so many politicians seem to do in other places. I do not think anyone can appreciate the problems involved (*Endurance*, political, etc.) until they have been down here and seen for themselves what goes on, both on our bases and on those of other countries, particularly Argentina. So Daddy has rather welcomed a "dull" day, in which to catch up on his reading and writing, both political and family.

We got a very amusing telex from Kathryn giving us welcome family "news", that all is well. Daddy sent his "greetings from 68° south 30° west". She replied "greetings from 53° north 40° east", or whatever London is. Our schedule has gone a bit haywire owing to the bad weather in Drake Passage and the pack ice up beyond Adelaide Island.

The Hydrographers are aboard again after drawing their pretty paths from which they produce really magnificent charts. There's a film on tonight. Daddy's going but I think I would rather go to bed and read.

9th March

I STILL feel a bit coldy, so am staying in. The plan was to fly to the Argentinian base at St. Martine, 40 miles away, but Tony Ellerbeck also has a cold. I think the choppers, their pilots, navigators and maintenance crews have been working very hard for the last few days, flying film crews, us, and yesterday the marines to Rothera to ski, though in fact most went by boat. I'm not surprised they were reluctant to take the choppers out again today. St. Martine being forty miles away it's not considered safe to fly there in one chopper, it's simply too far. One has to remember that this far south, if anything does go wrong, you either land in the water, where you have about ten minutes at the longest before you die of cold; or you land on an ice floe, which may crack; or you just try and find a flat bit of rocky mountain. Forty miles away there'd be little or no chance of a rescue, so I'm glad we didn't go.

I have spent a quiet day reading and knitting, it's been lovely and sunny but very cold. We went very close to a huge table top iceberg today, so that the film crew could get some marvellous shots. It wasn't a very tall one, but very impressive all the same.

This p.m. Daddy was interviewed on T.V. by Andy the Met Officer. It lasted about half an hour and was extremely good. Andy ask Daddy why he was here, how the House of Lords worked, and what he thought about the future of *Endurance.* It was an extremely good interview and I think everyone was interested. There are films (on cassettes) most days from 17.00, and news; also a newsletter comes round every morning with world news. We were sad to see that Rab Butler had died; he was a dear friend and neighbour when he was M.P. for Saffron Walden.

Daddy, Nick, and Mario, the Uruguayan commander on board, are busy discussing Antarctic politics, so I've left them to it, especially as Mario has an awful cold. This time next week we should be with Cindy and Annie. It will be marvellous to see them. I just hope the weather's fine.

10th March

WHEN it is fine, it's really lovely.

The hydrographers are having their last fling this morning, so Daddy went up on the bridge and I stayed below, as though sunny it was very cold. I am really trying to understand a bit about this unbelievable continent, quite hard work for me, and some of it's very technical, but when I can understand it, very interesting.

We flew into Rothera after dressing up in our goon suits (it takes longer to get dressed than to fly to Rothera) for the met officer to receive a degree he's got in Psychology from the Open University. He wanted to be filmed being handed his degree by Nick Barker at Rothera with *Endurance* in the background. Daddy insisted on my being photographed with a large and playful husky, and was photographed himself doing various

At last! Greeting Cindy at St. Andrew's Bay, photographed by Annie.

H.M.S. *Endurance* coming through the ''pack''. *Bob Mahoney*

Making friends with the St. Andrew's Bay penguins. *Annie Price*

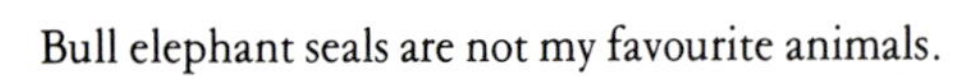

Bull elephant seals are not my favourite animals. *Annie Price*

other things, including congratulating Andy the Met Officer on his diploma.

We went for a short wander and found some lichen growing. The base commander said that one of the only two grasses found in Antarctica also grew there, so he rushed me off to find some. Unfortunately we couldn't find the patch, about four inches by six, two inches tall, said to be on the side of a small hill. But we did find several lichens, some red, some green, and two sorts of moss, one green, one browner; and one particular lichen, *Osnia Antarctica*, growing on a small piece of rock, which he gave me (how do I keep it cool enough?).

We then went up the hill to where they have built a stone cairn, surmounted by a white cross, with a plaque to the memory of the two young scientists who died last winter after falling down a crevasse. But then I saw Daddy in his goon suit signalling wildly to me to hurry, so I had to rush down and get into my suit, helmet, etc., and then out to the chopper to fly back. More photographs of me falling out of the chopper. I really must put a stop to it, it's becoming a bore and always in very unflattering circumstances.

It was a really wonderful afternoon. I can't believe my luck at being here and seeing it all. We've decided to put *Osnia* in the porthole ledge of our cabin. When it's rough the sea comes in a bit, it's always fairly cold so maybe it'll feel at home.

A. E. M. Barnes from ''flight' has done a spot of sponsored weight-lifting to raise money for the Peanut ward, which is the children's ward in a hospital at home especially devoted to burns. He lifted 320lb and has raised over £300 to endow at least two cots, a splendid effort.

We set off this p.m. going north up the side of Graham Land and in due course north-east to South Georgia. The icebergs were quite magnificent, more and larger then when we came down. It's noticeably colder, and small patches of pancake ice are forming, later to be pushed together and frozen into pack ice and finally fast ice, which goes from shore to shore. Fast ice occurs in and across the mouths of bays, between islands or round the shore, where in summer it may break off, leaving an ice-foot behind. At least I think that's what it is, it's all a bit beyond me.

We saw several seals, crab-eaters which don't eat crabs but like krill and are generally pale in colour. Weddell seals seemed larger, darker, and have white spots underneath, and I think I saw a leopard seal, but I'm not sure. One of the icebergs was in the shape of a huge ice-bridge, very dramatic. Another was just over a mile long, flat-topped, and sixty feet high.

11th March

TODAY started fine, but with a heavy sea and a strong north-easterly wind. We had a fairly rough time from Marguerite Bay until we were able to turn inside the shelter of the Argentine Islands (what an unfortunate name). We passed Faraday Base with *Bransfield* anchored in a bay, putting stores ashore and collecting summer personnel and specimens.

We then sailed to the Le Maire Straits, which we came down last time the other way, then in bright sunshine. What a difference! The wind is literally howling in the rigging, more powerful because it's funnelled down the narrow straits with

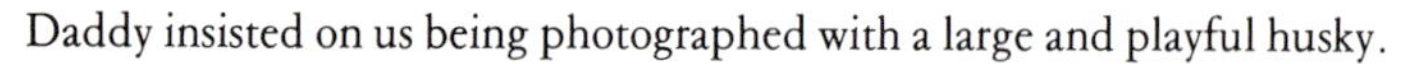

Daddy insisted on us being photographed with a large and playful husky.

high crags amd mountains, and steep ones at that, on either side. There is, oddly, very little snowfall in Antarctica and almost no rain. The snow, when it falls, is more like grains of fine hard white sand. At the moment any snow is being blown off the cliff face. Since we went through last month several new ''bergs'' have fallen from the ice-feet hanging on to the sides of the cliffs, and there are a lot of small ''growlers'' or tiny free-floating icebergs bobbing about; also a lot of what's called brash, small loose bits of ice which break off the cliff face when an ice foot falls into the water.

We appear to be steering into a dull mist but in fact it's the wind whipping up spray from the sea; you can see it coming, it's really very odd. It has given me my first real impression of what it must be like in winter here, though of course there would be ice everywhere. I don't think the Le Maire Straits will be passable much longer. Pack ice will start to form soon and eventually the whole strait will be held in an icy grip from shore to shore. Not nice smooth ice, as I had imagined, but ice formed by freezing winds which ruffle the surface of the sea with small waves as it freezes, so the eventual ''fast'' ice looks more like a vast sheet of corrugated iron, with ridges, not evenly spaced, and bergs trapped haphazardly here and there. You couldn't skate on it, or even drive a snow-cat, the surface is so deeply pitted.

The channel is widening out now, but there are still some handsome bergs in front. One of the potential dangers to ships is that many are not aground and can bear down on a ship very quickly. If they are flat-topped and have no under-water sticking-out bits and aren't too large, they nudge you and grind their way down the ship. But if they have spikey bits on top you can be fairly sure they have long tongues and feet below and if one (or more) gets under a ship, the iceberg can easily overturn it. They (the icebergs) weigh incredible weights. I can hear a small one (I hope) bumping its way down the side of the ship, leaving it ''marked'' with some of our red paint, no doubt.

The film team have been out in the bows facing into this biting wind and spray for the last hour. They really do earn their keep, they seem impervious to wind, weather and discomfort, not to say danger, in their quest for awe-inspiring photographs. Two sailors have also braved the elements and have been nonchalantly mending the biggest boat, the *James Caird*, who's somehow damaged herself, luckily above the water line. How

Sunset in the Le Maire Straits, seen from the bridge of *Endurance*.

they can work in 0° Centigrade in a howling gale, I simply cannot imagine. Luckily the sea is comparatively calm again due to the shelter of the islands, so at least we aren't pitching and rolling like we were this morning, when writing was really impossible.

As I write this a huge cloud of sea-spray has swept the window and driven even the intrepid film crew inside. The straits have widened out considerably now, the wind I'm told is 80 knots, or "force 11, gusting 12", and the sea looks grey, angry, and menacing. We should get into the lee of Anvers Island fairly soon, which will help to keep the swell down and make life more bearable.

12th March

WE ARE now among the South Shetland Islands, what you can see of them. It's still rather overcast, but luckily we can fly. We left at nine this morning, Nick and Daddy in one chopper, followed by Mario, the Uraguayan, and me in the second. There was a fair old gale blowing, no doors or seats, so a trifle cold, though the goon suits do keep you warm.

First we visited a Chilean naval base at Arturo Plat. Lovely buildings, every comfort, single-bedded rooms. We had a tour of the whole area; it's small, but very "homely", only two officers and ten men during the winter. We were as usual given a wonderful welcome, coffee and a special cake; every-one was so charming and friendly. We spent about an hour there and were presented with little bits of rock with lichen on. "Do you know what this is?" asked the base commander, pointing to the lichen. Amazingly (you all know my memory) I did remember and said "Yes, I do. *Osnia Antarctica*", which luckily pleased him no end. We now have three pieces of rock with *Osnia* residing on the ledge by our cabin porthole. I gather you just keep *Osnia* in the light, and cool, and put it in the fridge for a few hours once a week—just to remind it of home. Judging by the weather you seem to have been having at home, all I'll have to do is leave *Osnia* outside.

I'm very worried about reports coming in of heavy snowfalls in Wales. I do hope Roo and William* are all right and the babies, that's the only thing that's worrying me, being so far away from all my family. Daddy is marvellously phlegmatic and refuses even to think about it.

We left Arturo Plat and returned to *Endurance* to refuel, then took off again, this time with Daddy and I together, to the most enormous Chilean air force base at Rodolfo Marsh on King George Island. Also on the island is a small Argentine base, Presidente Frei, which is literally 500 yards from the Russian base of Bellingshausen, whilst over the top of the hills is the Polish base of Artowski.

I believe the poor Poles are in a pretty desperate state, short of food and supplies generally, and have had no mail or any boat in to relieve the men stuck there for a year. We were intending to go to Marsh for an hour and then on to Artowski, but things got a bit out of hand at Rodolfo Marsh. This is a big Chilean air force base with a most imposing runway which can take Hercules aircraft easily. Quite what the real purpose of this base is I am not sure; theoretically it can be used by aircraft of any nation, if I understood the "colonel" properly, but I very much doubt whether in fact any other nation does use it.

*A daughter and son-in-law.

We arrived slightly early, and caught them literally with their trousers down, changing into their smart uniforms. We were presented to so many colonels, commandants and commanders I got thoroughly confused. Most spoke some English and all were incredibly friendly. We had intended to stay for one hour and consequently were in scruffy flying clothes. I had no make-up with me, when to my horror I realised we were expected for a large and sumptuous luncheon, preceded by rounds of drinks. The Chileans clearly want to be our best friends.

There were also two smashing Brazilian girls there, a really attractive blonde with yards of thick hair, and the most marvellous figure, who is apparently a geologist; and a lovely dark girl whose job I never really fathomed. It was something to do with human ecology, psychology and social geography, if you can make anything of that. It was all the greatest fun, though we British felt slightly obvious in our jerseys and trousers, the flight command (pilots and navigators) in their sort of baby-grows they wear under their rubber flying suits. I did not even have time to comb my hair which had not been exactly coiffed by wearing a woolly hat and ear-muffs, and by walking to the base from the aircraft in a howling gale. But there it was, and they behaved as if we were the Queen and P.P.

Lunch was delicious, but the steaks were enormous. I felt I'd never get through mine, and eventually gave it up. We were given flags of the base, and super key-rings; and all the men were given huge bottles (4 litres) of wine, which were carefully carried on board the choppers. I was also given a holy picture at Arturo Plat of Our Lady of Mount Carmel. It's the only place where I've seen any religious pictures, statues, or even a rosary. No-one seems to have a chapel, or tiny place of prayer, or perhaps they didn't show us.

Our farewell at Marsh was utterly hilarious; to begin with the sight of us, particularly me, in our goon suits sent the girls into hysterics. Cameras were produced by everyone. (There are thirty men during winter and up to 200 during the summer and during the building of the airstrip and hangars.) We said our goodbyes. Everyone, male and female, kissed me, and suddenly our navigator popped up behind me, kissed me and said "goodbye ma'am", which brought the house down. Daddy was photographed with his arms round both Brazilian beauties. I wish I could get a copy of that. It would give *Private Eye* something to write about.

We had a super flight back, taking off absolutely together, a sort of minor show of expertise by the "Flight". The captain embarked whilst we circled the ship, and then we landed as the other Wasp took off again. I sat on the outside flying back, it was super, though with no doors you do feel awfully near to falling out when the aicraft turns your way, even though you know you're firmly strapped in.

No sooner had we got back to our cabin than they called down from the bridge that the tiny 300-ton *Hero*, an American merchant ship connected with the Antarctic bases and scientists, was churning through the swell. She'd just been to Artowski

The *Hero* is a really splendid sight . . . busily going about in a cheeky fashion when larger ships are groaning and rolling or heaving to.

with food for the Poles. Some of them have been there for seventeen months, it seems, and no-one quite knows what's going to happen next. I feel so sorry for them, it must be awful for them, cut off from their families, with Poland in the turmoil it's in at the moment.

The *Hero* is a really splendid sight. She's painted green and even has two red-brown sails. She looks like a cheeky little cockney flower girl among the more staid *Endurance*, *Glacier*, *Bransfield* and *John Biscoe*. Her captain, Lenny, a Belgian-American, is a real character, taking his little ship, which reminds me of a tug in some ways, or even a trawler, gaily across Drake Passage in all weathers, busily going about in a cheeky fashion when larger ships are groaning and rolling or heaving to. He's like one of the old sailing skippers, thumbing his nose at the staider captains, and gaily going on where they fear to sail.

The sun's come out, I do hope it clears up when we're at South Georgia. We should arrive on Monday, weather permitting. But we still have Drake Passage to cross (five hundred miles) and the forecast is "Rough", so I may not write up any more if it gets too lively. I miss you all dreadfully. I think two weeks is about the limit of my ability to survive without contact with my family. I'll never learn, but this has been such a superb trip I'll never ever forget it, nor the laughs we've had, which have been many.

I've just realised I've said nothing about Marsh Base itself. It was built two years ago, and finished last year. It's the most fabulous wooden building, apart from the hangars and runway. It was the only station, or base, which we were not shown over, so I presume the scientific studies done there are very limited, if any, but they do have foreign scientists, French, German, Brazilian, etc. I did, however, get a small insight into the layout. It's all on one floor, raised off the ground. The bedrooms are really lush, beds not bunks, some single, some twin-bedded, and at least one double plus loo and basin. The whole place is wood-lined, with big double-glazed windows. It's rather hard to describe really, as it's just a long wooden hut from the outside, but really rather lavish inside.

The colonel of Marsh Base told me that they were a sort of huge reception centre of meterological data from bases all round the South Pole, not just their own, but from Amundsen-Scott base on the South Pole and the "other side". This data was then sent to Santiago, and then to Boston, U.S.A. The data reached Boston from Marsh in four hours. This could be incorrect, as my knowledge of met is nil, and the colonel's English was limited. But this is what I understood.

13th March

WHAT might have been a dull day, as we were at sea, turned out to be the greatest fun. Daddy did a lot of work in the morning, and we then went down by invitation to the Senior Ratings' Mess, for a drink before lunch. They are a marvellous bunch, and most of them know "C and A".

We stayed there talking and laughing until well after one

o'clock, when Daddy thought we shouldn't keep the captain waiting for his lunch any longer. We had some good laughs, and one chap showed me some superb slides of St. Andrew's Bay where "C and A's" hut is, all among the penguins and elephant seals. The chaps, most of them, were very concerned about the future of *Endurance*, as we all are, and the ones who have only done one year, and therefore could do another, are finding the uncertainty very worrying. Their concern for the whole thing came over very strongly.

Saturday night at sea was dinner in the wardroom, not quite long dresses, but my one and only cocktail sort of dress. It was most amusing, everything under the sun was discussed, and Bill Hurst, the Mess President, welcomed us. It was great fun and a privilege to be there. Luckily *Endurance* wasn't rolling very much, but enough for the table to move left to right and back again, so one's plate was constantly moving, but luckily not the chairs. Bill, the President, is a keen supporter of S.D.P. and thinks they'll get in next time; I'm not so sure. We don't really get much news here apart from headlines, so I've no idea what's been going on on the political front beyond a brief outline of the Budget.

After dinner the captain suggested liar dice. I've never played before and simply couldn't grasp the principle at all. Daddy was marvellous and nobly plunged in, though I don't think he'd ever played before, but he catches on to those sort of games so quickly. I felt an absolute fool not understanding what was going on in the least. I wish I had a better "card" or "dice" head, it's so embarrassing when one can't play. So ended a peaceful but amusing day.

14th March

SUNDAY, so church in the seamens' dining room. This time we had chairs, though the ship is still rolling quite enough for me. The service was being shot for the film that is being made of *Endurance*. As Nick came in he whispered to me "This is the first time I've ever been wired up as a parson".

The service was very nice, four rousing hymns, prayers, and a reading, very simple but nevertheless sincere. As we went out, Master at Arms said to me "The first time we've had a soprano in the *Endurance*". I'd forgotten the filming and sound were going on.

It seems amazing to think that we shall actually see ''C and A'' tomorrow, hopefully in the morning. The sea is fairly calm, so we might be making good time. We've been looking for whales up on the bridge, but none in sight. The radar has gone completely haywire, so the ''sparks'' are tearing their hair out and have wires and fuses all over the deck.

It seems unbelievable that our fantastic holiday is nearly over, it seems to have gone like a flash. This is our third Sunday on board. We seem to have done so much and seen so much, it's hard to take it all in. I only hope my photographs come out, though with professional photographers clicking away at every opportunity there will be no lack of record of superb quality.

We spent a very instructive and interesting afternoon in the hydrographers' room, where they showed us all the work done during the time that they were at Rothera, both on their own with just the *James Caird* and when on *Endurance*. It really was very intriguing, meticulously done, echo-sounding every 100 metres working in straight or curved lines 250 metres apart. From the tiny figures sea charts are built up at Cambridge and the charts are then sold world-wide.

This evening more than thirty icebergs came up on the radar, but unfortunately not visible to the naked eye even with image intensifier glasses which enable you to see things at night. We watched for a while, then went to bed. At midnight apparently there were more than a hundred bergs within twelve miles of us, and you could see some, but I was too sleepy to stay up. We shall see Cindy and Annie at South Georgia tomorrow. I can hardly wait, having come half way across the world to see them in their little hut.

South Georgia

15th March

THE great day has dawned, sadly dull and damp. We were due to fly out at nine, but the "Helo" developed oil pressure trouble, so Daddy and I finally got off at 10.30. At 9.30 I spoke to Cindy on the radio, it was marvellous to hear her voice. We finally got off, and it was only a short flight from Royal Bay to St. Andrew's Bay. On the way I took photographs of herds of reindeer on the mountains.

And then there they were, two tiny figures armed with cameras, a tiny hut, and a huge Union Jack doing its best to fly in the damp windless conditions. I had my camera out, too, and photographed them as well. Hope the pictures come out.

We had a rapturous welcome. Both girls looked wonderful, Cindy much better than usual, and Annie her usual blooming self. Goodness, it was good to see them. We took our awful orange suits off to return them to the "Helo", which was going back to *Endurance* to fetch in the film crew, who tactfully left us alone and filmed at a distance the penguin colony and seals.

The hut is tiny but superbly clean and neat and tidy. Two bunk beds run the width of the end wall. Two windows opposite each other, a tiny table or shelf along the dividing wall, a chair, a stool and a door. That's their living quarters. Book shelves right up above the bunk, heaven knows where their clothes are. Next comes a tiny kitchen with two primuses, and shelves for perishables or stores in use. Through this to the lobby, where coats are hung, cameras, etc. And that's all! 12 feet by 7 feet 6 inches at the most.

Outside the front door (which locks, luckily!) is a platform, and on it the loo, built by *Endurance's* carpenters, a wooden throne, with wooden cistern and a ball and chain hanging from it. On the seaward side of the hut is a huge red tarpaulin where all the food, in tins of course, is kept; the tarpaulin weighted down with huge stones. Then round to the end opposite to the front door, a green tarpaulin where they keep heaven knows what—I think suitcases, skirts and shirts and probably fuel (paraffin for the tilley, and fuel for the primus stoves).

"C and A" waiting for the chopper to land near their hut at St. Andrew's Bay.

There were penguins everywhere, very tame once the choppers had gone. They are madly inquisitive and poke their noses into everything. The hut isn't amongst the main colony (far too smelly) but there must be 20-30,000 in the bay. King penguins are lovely birds, about 3 feet tall, with lovely yellow markings behind their ears (if they have any) and down their chest a little way, with an orange-red slash on the lower beak.

We were immediately dragged off to see some albatross chicks (light mantled sooty), elephant seals, and a couple of extremely nasty vicious fur seals. Daddy went with Cindy while Annie and I photographed elephant seals. Then I tried to climb what appeared to be a sheer cliff-face, luckily covered in tussock grass, to see the chicks. I hate heights and I kept putting my foot in a hole; the journey up was hilarious, but with Cindy pulling and

Annie pushing I managed, and the chick was most obliging and posed for me. It even consented to nibble my gloves. We then saw another chick with its parents who were also quite unafraid and let me photograph them. The journey down was rather slippery but fairly safely negotiated.

We then had a huge drink, *Tio Pepe* no less, which Annie had hoarded for me. Whisky for Pa. We then opened our "packed lunches" and the girls fell upon our sandwiches and cold sausages with cries of "bread! sausages!" So they had our lunch and we had their biscuits and cheese; excellent, but I can see you would get pretty bored with it after six months.

After lunch we donned boots and anoraks and walked over to the penguin colony. This sounds simple enough but it involved crossing a very slippery glacier with nasty cracks in it, and several huge holes, where the ice had just caved in or melted for no apparent reason. They were very impressive holes, the ice must have been two metres thick, but one couldn't help wondering where the next hole was going to appear. Then we walked up a shale-covered bit of glacier with the melt stream hurling itself seawards in a swirl of floodwater. This particular glacier is a horrid pale tawny grey colour, as so much shale and muck has come down from the mountains.

Being sub-Antarctic it's totally different from anything we'd seen up till now. Grass grows on the lower slopes and water runs from the glaciers, some of which are receding rather fast. This particular one at St. Andrew's Bay has gone back ten feet in the last few months. The landscape, apart from the glaciers, looks very much like Ardvar*, except that there is more shale or scree on the slopes, and the green vegetation is confined to the lower slopes.

I found eight or nine different mosses but have no book of sub-Antarctic plants. Also a very common weed the reindeer graze, called Echina (don't know how you spell it).

We finally reached the penguin colony after I'd fallen over three times, Annie once and Daddy once. It was unbelievable, thousands and thousands of penguins, adults and almost adult; still fluffy, quite small chicks; and even some eggs. King penguins lay two eggs every three years for some extraordinary reason. They lay their eggs and incubate them on their feet, a flap of skin folding down from their tummies to cover the egg

*Where the family used to go in Sutherland.

There were penguins everywhere, they are madly inquisitive and poke their noses into everything.

and presumably keep it warm. They look very odd incubating their eggs, as they appear to have no feet, the flap of skin coming right to the ground. It's rather sad really, this odd way of laying eggs so haphazardly. I believe it's because the chicks take so long to grow up enough to fend for themselves, but whatever the reason the late-hatched chicks have little or no chance of surviving the winter, and usually die of cold or starvation. It all seems so sad and so ill arranged. There is, of course, the added peril of skuas and sheathbills taking the eggs. The skuas are large ugly-looking brown birds with a decidely nasty look in their eyes. The sheathbills are about the size of a wood pigeon or slightly smaller, white, and look rather sweet. How appearances can lie; they are just as predatory as the skuas, though I don't think they'd take a penguin chick like the skuas do.

We had a really wonderful afternoon and returned by way of the beach, though we had to climb back up across the glacier again as the melt stream was too deep. We had a cup of tea and then saw the Gemini (rubber dinghy) coming to us, or so we thought. Lights began flashing from *Endurance* so Cindy ran back to her radio but they didn't answer her. Eventually Daddy strode purposefully towards the Gemini and told it where the only landing place was and to come in. We clambered over rocks, seals and heaven knows what and got in the boat. What we didn't know until later was that the Gemini was supposed to pick up a party of sailors and the film crew first, the choppers having shut down for the day, and then fetch us. Thank heaven we went first, as on their return journey the engine fell off the Gemini, which drifted away with two marines aboard. So the whaler had to be hurriedly launched to fetch the, by now, rather alarmed sailors and a very wet film crew, who had tried to cross the melt stream. However finally all were safely gathered in, and "C and A" proceeded to the sick bay, where they were sleeping, to have their first hot shower since October.

Daddy gave a buffet party that night in the wardroom to thank the officers for their unfailing help and kindness to us on our holiday. It really was quite a party. "C and A" knew everyone, of course, and when I left at 11.30 the party was going strong.

During the morning *Endurance* had airlifted the Joint Services Expedition off Royal Bay, where they had been doing what Dick Laws rudely refers to as "Boy Scout" exercises. They have been climbing mountains and glaciers and doing a certain amount of scientific work, also some filming of Annie and Cindy for Cindy's film. In my view the expeditions do show some initiative and sense of adventure, which can't be bad, and the members were either sponsored or paid their own way.

So ended a really memorable day, I can hardly believe we've actually come across the world (nearly) to see "C and A" and have achieved it; it's all been utterly fantastic.

16th March

CINDY and Pa were airlifted back to St. Andrew's Bay, as they wanted to talk shop, to see if any more "shots" were required, and to look over her notes. So Annie and I went to Grytviken, where *Endurance* anchored and we went ashore by boat. We had lunch at Shackleton House, the H.Q. of B.A.S. on South Georgia. It's a superb building which is, apparently, being closed in a month or two when the new house is finished.

After lunch we walked round to the old whaling base of Grytviken. It was rather an eerie feeling walking among the deserted wooden buildings, rusting boilers, anchor chains and all the paraphernalia of a whaling station. It had been a whaling station for a great number of years, and was only given up in 1964 (I think) when the whaling industry became uneconomic owing to the gross over-killing of whales. The huts, equipment, etc. were all left in working order as the whalers, Norwegians mostly, expected to return there in a season or two. Alas for them, but luckily for the whales, they have never returned.

The town has an extraordinary feeling, like a ghost town; you feel you might meet some whalers round any corner. There are two whaling ships (iron ones) half sunken by the rotting wooden jetty, which is really more a huge platform where they hauled the whales up, ready to winch them up ramps to the various departments.

We walked right through the town and out to the cemetery where, among others, Sir Ernest Shackleton of Antarctic fame lies buried. He died, sadly, on 5th January, 1922, of a heart attack on his way to try another Antarctic expedition, and was buried at Grytviken.

Most of the graves are of Norwegians, but one or two are of Englishmen, who seem to have died at sea or were by chance at Grytviken. There are many tributes to Shackleton round his grave. After visiting the cemetery we saw the old cinema, which

There are two whaling ships (iron ones) half sunken by the rotting wooden jetty.

Playing with a light-mantled sooty albatross chick on its nest in South Georgia.
Annie Price

Taking it easy on one of the jetties of the abandoned whaling station at Grytviken.
Annie Price

Inside the whalers' church at Grytviken, with the cob-webby Christmas tree still standing from the previous year's carol service. *M.B.*

Endurance's victorious football team with their trophy after the vital game at Port Stanley. *M.B.*

is unfortunately falling down, and we were given the key of the chapel. This was built of wood in 1913, very simple, Lutheran in concept, and is used at Christmas for a carol service. It has a wonderful atmosphere of peace and serenity, very plain and simple, no statues, no holy pictures. Plain, obviously hand-made, unvarnished pews, enough to seat between sixty and a hundred, I should think. The altar rail is in a gentle curve, the altar a plain "table" with tall gold-painted candlesticks either side. Between the candlesticks is a silver painted panel with the text from St. Matthew in gold letters:

> Come unto Me
> All ye who are weary
> And are heavy laden
> And I will give you rest. Mat 11 28

Above this is a plain gold-painted cross, and right at the top a quarter monstrance or a rising sun, a gold quarter circle with

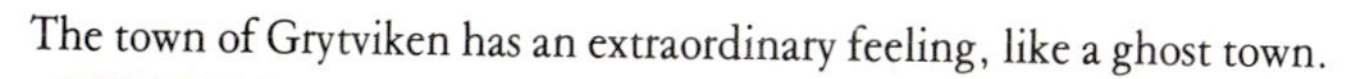

The town of Grytviken has an extraordinary feeling, like a ghost town.

rays spreading out of it. It was all very simple but moving, and it had the smell of a not very often used church. Up in the organ loft was a small organ, and some church music, a Norwegian carol service of 1960, an English carol service of the 1970s, a Russian prayer book and a Roman missal. Perhaps the church was interdenominational among those old whalers. The Christmas tree was still standing, rather cob-webby, from last Christmas's carol service, and two boards were inscribed in Norwegian:

Before the Gospel
. . .
. . .
After the Gospel

the space between being for the numbers of the various hymns or psalms.

After we left the church, it was time to go back to *Endurance* and sadly to return Annie to St. Andrew's Bay and for me to go to say goodbye to Cindy. As we were more than fifteen miles from St. Andrew's Bay we had to take both choppers, in case one got into trouble. So Annie set off first, and then me, clutching a precious loaf of bread for them. I flew with pilot Tim Fielding. We flew over a tremendously crevassed and ugly-looking glacier, and then between two mountain peaks, before coming down into the bay. It was really lovely, as the day had cleared up and the sun was shining. All the same I felt we were flying over a very grim and forbidding land that would preserve its secrets with all its might.

When I landed I found that Cindy had taken off in helo 435 to do some last-minute aerial photography which hadn't been possible before owing to the low cloud base.

At last it was time to say goodbye. We hugged each other and reminded each other it would be only another five weeks before we meet again. They are due to be picked up on 20th April, in four weeks time. Then Daddy got into his chopper and I into mine, and in formation we took off and circled the bay, the girls looking to me very small and rather forlorn, waving their handkerchiefs. But in fact they were probably longing to get back into their own routine, make supper and go to bed surrounded by the familiar sounds of penguins and elephant seals.

Our flight back was fantastic, flying side by side over the mountains, valleys and glaciers and finally over the sea to

Endurance, which had already weighed anchor and was sailing towards the Falkland Islands.

So ended the most wonderful and memorable two days. I don't know of any other elderly parents lucky enough to visit their daughter and adopted daughter at the other end of the world, in such comfort, and with such efficiency and speed. It is terribly sad to think that the "wild" part is over, and from now on we are in "civilized" parts again.

I felt very sad leaving Cindy. It truly is another world out here. Harsh, unpredictable and dangerous it may be, but for me the Antarctic holds a charm I shall never forget, and I for one will regret very much the inevitable "development" of what must be almost the last vast area of natural environment. I know we saw it in an enormously civilized way, by air and sea, warm cabins, good food and drink, but we were both aware of the sense of isolation.

Long may it last. It is such a wonderful and awe-inspiring part of the world it seems to put man where he belongs here, on a very low plane—and utterly defenceless against the devastating power of nature in the form of icebergs and glaciers, and the sheer size and magnificence of them.

17th March

THIS morning we were invited to the forecastle (fo'c'sle to you) by "the Buffer", a splendid chap, Petty Officer Pearson, to have coffee with them at 9.30. By 9 a.m. it was decidedly rough, so the M.O. asked if we wanted to cancel it, but no way. Daddy and I were undaunted and sallied forth to the fo'c'sle.

It was the greatest fun. Ten seamen, who man the boats and generally maintain them, one a Falkland Islander, or "Kelper" as they call them, another, Taffy Johns, from near Bridgend (South Wales). We had a great time sitting among the coiled ropes, all neatly stowed away, with hooks, pulleys, and all the tools one might need at any time. Biscuits were produced in our honour, and we had a really amusing hour's talk drinking coffee. The crash of the ship's bows as she hit each wave was really impressive (the sea is now "rough") but we both enjoyed ourselves enormously.

I have just been down to the galley to thank the head cook, P. O. Stewart, for such a delicious buffet dinner on Monday night.

It is such a wonderful and awe-inspiring part of the world it seems to put man where he belongs.

The film crew are all over the place with wires trailing everywhere, filming a mock "briefing".

This evening we are doling out crates of beer to the various decks by way of thanks for all their kindness to us on our trip. Daddy is due to go on yet another T.V. interview tonight, this time with Andy Lockett and Nick Barker. Rather him than me. Then we have the two leaders of the Joint Services Expedition for drinks and to thank them for taking the film of "C and A", and generally going over to see that they were all right.

Tomorrow we have at sea. I hope it's not too rough, it makes reading or writing a chore, though luckily we are pitching and not rolling. Then on Thursday we arrive in Stanley, and our wonderful holiday is nearly over. It's gone in a flash.

I telephoned Nicky* one evening by satellite to ask about Eleanor's efforts at Ascot. I was so thrilled she had got in, well done her. The line was amazingly clear, I couldn't believe we

*Nicola Sykes, an elder daughter.

were speaking over 8,000 miles. I hear Tim has gone to Canada and New York, and will be home the same day as us. Good. I am longing to see you all, and hear all your news. We also telephoned Roo as we had reports of bad snow-storms in Wales but luckily they were all right in that way, but had awful rain and gales. Poor things, they'd be better off here.

18th March

THE sea was so rough writing was almost impossible. Really huge waves, and the wind coming head on. Quite a day, a few faces absent. We spent a quiet day tidying up before arriving at Stanley tomorrow, as we're staying the night at G.H., then back on board Saturday night.

In the evening we went down to the wardroom at the invitation of the J.S.E. (Joint Services Expedition) officers. They were really a most interesting bunch, soldiers, sailors and marines. All the officers at any rate were experienced in their own fields; mountaineering, glaciology, marine biology, etc. They were very interesting about ice-fish which, having no blood in the accepted sense, are quite transparent. They seem to have a sort of saline solution in their veins, and they get oxygen from the sea-water under the ice. At least I think that's what happens, but I don't think anyone knows exactly, which is why the ice-fish are being sent to Bangor University, suitably embalmed (the fish, not the university), where they can be studied in more depth.

The J.S.E. seem to have enjoyed their three-month adventure very much, though I would not have fancied living in conditions such as they did. Their "rations", however, were very superior to those Cindy got from the marines, so a bit of swapping went on. They walked over from Royal Bay to St. Andrew's occasionally with extra goodies.

So we arrive at Stanley tomorrow. I have a huge pile of mail from Cindy for her friends in Stanley and requests for stamps from Annie. The Falkland Islands make a lot of money on first day cover stamps and they really are lovely. I have collected all I can, also the J.S.E. stamp and of course Cindy's St. Andrew's Bay. Only six more days before we get to Montevideo and start our rather long flight home. I suppose all good things must come to an end, and I am really longing to see you all again.

Storm clouds

19th March

We have arrived off Stanley. It is one of the most beautiful days you can imagine, blue sky, fluffy white clouds, calm blue sea, a welcome change since yesterday. We packed our cases for one night's stay at G.H., which seems to require nearly all one's clothes, bar foul weather gear and sea-boots.

Intense excitement at about 11.30; reports of an Argentine Lear jet in trouble (undercarriage wouldn't descend) over Stanley. Also reports of another jet, also Argentine, in support. I pulled Nick's leg and said we'd obviously arrived as the invasion had started. I think he (Nick) was quite excited.

However, all was explained by the resident marine major who arrived on board by chopper. The jet had been expected and was now all right, so all the excitement died down.

We also heard that an Argentinian C130 Hercules had suddenly landed at Port Stanley, stayed a short time and then taken off again. Cindy also told us it had been buzzing about over South Georgia.

It's so lovely here, the islands lying green and grey in the sun, it's hard to believe that acrimony and discord surround them. The islands were obviously meant for peaceful occupation, sheep farming and such pursuits, not Argentine naval bases. The choppers are busy transporting hydrographers to Berkeley Sound to do yet more survey work; they really are a dedicated race. The flight crews are also going ashore at Green Patch to help herd sheep, by chopper, rather a novel idea. They are all being left behind until the *Endurance* returns from Montevideo with a new contingent of Royal Marines, to take over from the Marines who've been here now for a year. We shall be going to Montevideo in *Endurance*.

It will be really sad saying goodbye to all the chaps we've met, flown with and generally passed the time of day with this last month. Although feeding with the captain, we have got to know the members of the wardroom so well. We seem to have got to know most of them on board. I suppose after the captain, we've got to know the doctor and the chopper pilots best, as we've been with them much more, and of course Francis

Ponsonby; but the whole ship's company have been so friendly I shall never forget their kindness to me personally.

On arrival at Stanley, we were met by Rex Hunt. The work boat again wouldn't start so we transferred to a sort of tug, the *Lively*. Don was waiting for us with the maroon taxi. Owing to the head winds and rough sea we were rather late, so we weren't able to post the letters, cards, etc. However as most of the Stanley letters (from "C and A") were local, they went by hand anyway.

Nick and Bill came for dinner, and during dinner we seemed to become part of a really dreadful "James Bond" film.

I must explain that a certain Argentine "gentleman" named Davidoff has obtained rights from a British firm (who claim they could get no offers from Britain) to salvage the "scrap iron", boilers, sheets of metal, anchors, etc, which I saw still lying about the old whaling stations of Grytviken, Leith, Husvik and Stromness. This Davidoff has been under Her Majesty's Government's eye, in the shape of Nick and Rex Hunt, for some time, as his "salvaging" activities seemed to be of a somewhat dubious nature, and Argentine naval ships had been used to bring him to the whaling station.

It's all rather complicated, but Argentina claims South Georgia as hers, as well as the Falklands. H.M.G. remain firm that South Georgia is a dependency and consequently demand that "foreigners" register their presence at Grytviken, with a "magistrate" in the person of the B.A.S. base commander. Now for the James Bond bit.

During dinner a coded message is handed to Rex. Hurried message sent to decoder, who arrives, panting, on a bicycle. Code being used is unfamiliar, so dinner is finished before message is decoded. Horror of horrors, a small party of B.A.S. scientists at Leith quietly pursuing their own thing are suddenly confronted by an Argentine naval ship flying the Argentine flag, and apparently disembarking about twenty men, some in uniform. Very correctly B.A.S. chaps asked them what they wanted, or words to that effect. They were working for Davidoff and "had permission from British Embassy in B.A." All very friendly. They were then asked to please go and register at Grytviken on entering South Georgia—no comment. A hurried call was then sent to Grytviken, who sent off coded message to Stanley.

Speculation now ran high at G.H., messages were sent to London and B.A., marked urgent, and the light of battle glinted in Nick's eye, as well as in Rex's. Rex has twice warned Davidoff not to go to Leith before "registering" at Grytviken. The Embassy in B.A. seems to be out of line.

20th March

WE ALL went to bed last night in a fever of excitement. Were the Argentines trying to establish a base or settlement in South Georgia, under cover of Davidoff's "salvage" contract? By the following morning Nick was back again, and answers and further messages were flying about.

The Argentines were still at Leith but had taken down their flag. The ship seemed to have vanished (probably in a neighbouring bay).

The afternoon was, in true British naval tradition, given over to football, a vital game between *Endurance* and Stanley. *Endurance* only had to draw to win the shield, which they've never done before. You've never seen anything like it. Davidoff, Argentines, illegal settlements were all forgotten as we cheered or booed the two teams, playing like demons in a howling gale, on a pitch sloping alarmingly towards the sea. Luckily the gale was from the sea, so no divers had to be called out to rescue the ball. If the wind hadn't prevented any decent football being played it would have been a good match. As it was we yelled ourselves hoarse, nearly got blown away, froze quietly about our hands, feet and ears, and finally saw *Endurance* win the shield for the first time 6-4. The excitement was quite as great as at a cup final.

After that we came down to earth with a bump, to more James Bond. More secret signals were received and sent, protests from H.M. Ambassador to B.A. (fat lot of good that will do), and to our intense surprise we got no end of a positive reaction from London. At 20.00 approx. an officer from *Endurance* in full rig arrived at the Stewarts' house, where we were all having a supper party, with the latest report from London. *Endurance* to return to South Georgia forthwith and investigate. At long last, after years, a positive reaction to Argentina seeing how far she could go without getting her hand smacked.

It is very sad for us though, as of course we'll have to leave *Endurance*. Apart from their not wanting civilians on board, other than the camera crew, who are employed by M.O.D., if *Endurance* is delayed in South Georgia we'll miss our plane home. Trust us to get mixed up in spy and counter-spy. We are staying tonight at G.H. and go aboard *Endurance* to collect our luggage at seven tomorrow morning, Sunday.

21st March

VERY sadly we went aboard *Endurance* to pack our luggage and take leave of everyone. It really was like leaving home. In the flurry of the moment I have left all my ''slops'' behind, also a particularly precious but revolting-looking bottle with krill in it swimming in formalin. I wonder what else I've left. We came back amid an appropriate drizzle with Mario, the Uruguayan naval commander, and went off to mass together.

On our return Rex told us he'd been through to Grytviken, who reported that at Leith their ''spies'' said that there were now about fifty Argentines milling about with the ship back in view. All still very friendly, but refusing to go to Grytviken for ''clearance''.

At lunch Rex had a signal from B.A. saying that the Argentine Foreign Minister was very embarrassed by it all, almost apologised, and whilst disclaiming all responsibility for the Argentines at Leith, promised their withdrawal today. I wonder what will happen.

It's sad for us as we should have been going up to Montevideo with *Endurance* this morning, and then flying on to Rio. I had been told Rio was a much better shopping centre than B.A. I've no ''mementoes'' for anyone and heaven knows if I'll ever get to Rio now except in transit.

Endurance has been told to pretend to be proceeding to Montevideo, so presumably we will get no signals from her. If only it all blows over and she can come back here, but as each hour passes our chances of getting to Montevideo in time to catch our plane with *Endurance* fade; and alas, we shall have to go back with that awful LADE, if we can get on, and if they will accept all our luggage.

It is becoming rather a worry, the whole thing. Oh dear, why did it have to go wrong; we were having such a lovely time and would have got back in time to see Mops, Vicky, John, Amanda and Sarah*, before they fly out on the 28th. How I wish *Endurance* would appear again out over the hills in the harbour. I have been rather worried too about Annie and Cindy, but am

*Daughters and grandchildren.

assured that they are a long way from Leith and will be quite all right. B.A.S. know they are there and if anything untoward happens I feel sure *Endurance* will go in and pick them up. What a to-do.

22nd March

"JAMES BOND" continues with signals flying in and out from B.A. and Grytviken. No news from *Endurance*. I only hope she's still steaming full ahead to South Georgia and some twit in London hasn't ordered her to resume her previous course to Montevideo. Daddy and Rex are to be seen with stern faces consulting telex signals, and rumours are now flying about—I'm not joking—that the Argentines have invaded the Falklands! Well, so far I haven't noticed them. Maybe I am speaking too soon! Or I am not looking in the right direction.

We went down with Mario, the Uruguayan commander from *Endurance*, who is now staying here, to book flights on LADE to B.A. next Wednesday. I hope to heavens they don't cancel the flight, there is only one a week. We shall just have to wait and see if it comes in tomorrow.

The reports from Grytviken say that there are still five or six men, a launch and a landing craft at Leith, so we are all wondering whether the *Bahia Buen Suceso** has actually left, or is merely standing by round in another bay. The wretched B.A.S. boys at Grytviken (there are only ten of them) have a seven-hour walk to Leith, so they seem to have set up an observation post somewhere. It's rather hard luck on them, they are scientists, not policemen.

If any Argentines are still at Leith tomorrow morning, and if *Endurance* hasn't been diverted, they should get a nasty shock on Tuesday, or possibly Wednesday, when *Endurance* arrives. At least the choppers will be able to go all over the island to see whether *Buen Sucesco* is still in hiding. It all has a slightly unbelievable air about it, not least being that *Endurance* is so slow, it takes her three days to get to South Georgia, even with a following wind.

A press statement has been issued both here and in England, so I hope no-one is getting anxious about "C and A", or even us. But you'll probably not see the statement. So far no-one's been on to Daddy, though the local *Daily Express* overseas

*An Argentine Navy transport which had been employed to land the "scrap merchants".

"snippet" correspondent has contacted the Governor and been given a fairly guarded statement.

23rd March

YESTERDAY Daddy sent off a private and fairly strongly worded "scrambled" message to Lord Carrington advising no mealy-mouthed measures, and to our delight this a.m. came confirmation from London that *Endurance* is to proceed with all speed (12 knots at the most) to Leith and take the Argentines (if there are any left there still) on board. It's now ceased to be James Bond, and at long last H.M.G. is actually doing something. I only hope our Ambassador in B.A., who is all for not upsetting the Argentines, isn't having a heart attack.

Reports of a French yacht in Leith harbour caused a stir until I said I'd seen a French yacht, the *Cinq gars pour*, in Grytviken on Tuesday. I was able to describe her, registered Nantes, black hull, etc., and had been told there were three Frenchmen aboard her. Apparently Grytviken confirmed this but added that *Cinq gars pour* had been expressly forbidden to go into Leith harbour.

A lunchtime rumour, so far unconfirmed, says that the yacht had put into Leith because the Argentine launch had gone adrift, and *Cinq gars pour* had rescued her; we'll see.

One rather amusing thing happened here on Saturday night, which I forgot to mention in the excitement over South Georgia. The LADE (Argentine Air Force air line) office was broken into (a key was used, which gives rise to some speculation), the Argentine flag had a Union Jack pasted over it and the words TIT FOR TAT were sprayed in white paint on the window. The LADE office is staffed by Argentines, who rather naturally were totally at a loss as to what Tit for Tat meant. A hurried search through a Spanish-English dictionary must have been even more confusing. The mind rather boggles at the permutations of a dictionary definition of Tit and Tat!

The reason for the flag-changing appears to be that the Argentine radio put out a statement on Saturday that the Argentine flag had been put up at Leith. This was before H.E. (Rex) was informed by B.A.S. As the Argentine government denied all knowledge of the flag waving and professed themselves totally uninvolved in the affair, how did the Argentine radio get to know and broadcast the incident? The

Argentine government is obviously lying through its teeth, and although maybe not necessarily responsible for the landing, must have known. Certainly their Navy did.

I wonder whether ''C and A'' have heard yet. They talk to Grytviken every night, but may not have been told, as it's all been a bit cloak and dagger. If they did know I'll bet they are both at the top of Heine glacier with binoculars, scanning the horizon, and have hoisted their Union Jack. I wouldn't put it past them. They've probably painted Union Jacks on the elephant seals too, if they can find any friendly ones.

Today's LADE flight has landed, with H.E.'s son on board, for the return flight tomorrow. I only hope we don't get any awkwardness tomorrow, as *Endurance* should by then have arrived at Leith. They may of course find everyone gone. I only hope an Argentine gunboat isn't lying around. They could outgun *Endurance* in five minutes, but I doubt they'd risk it. It would be an act of war.

If it wasn't for my longing to see Mops and family and Vicky I wish we could stay and hear the end of the saga, but no doubt Daddy having got himself well and truly involved will know what is going on.

We have just had a signal from Nick, sent up from the marine barracks, saying they will be in touch with ''C and A'' and will take them off if Nick B feels the situation calls for it.

So our little trip, courtesy of H.M. Navy, has really turned into an extraordinary story, certainly one I shall never forget. It has been fascinating being, if not at the centre of things, at least on the side-lines and very keen observers. I only hope B.A.S. personnel will get the credit they deserve for their acute observation and swift action, not to mention these days of sustained observation under anything but comfortable conditions. I'll bet they'll be glad to see *Endurance*, whether there are any Argentines left or not.

My main worry now is whether we'll get into and out of Argentina tomorrow. We hope to fly straight on to Brazil, all being well.

I sent a birthday telegram to Roo for 24th and Edward for 25th. Rather mundane requests, amidst all the secret signals flying to and from the Cable and Wireless office.

We have yet another party tonight, the J.S.E. are throwing one at the marine barracks and the Pitalugas from Salvador are giving a send-off party for their older son, who leaves tomorrow for New Zealand, where's he's doing three one-year diploma courses (not all at once, one a year) before returning to Salvador. One's on farm management, one's on sheep farming, and one's on wool. There is no arable here, and New Zealand appears to be the only place where he can do these three courses. I hope the party doesn't go on too late, we have to be at the airport by 07.00. Let's hope the flight goes off smoothly.

Have just heard that *Endurance* is to go into Grytviken and Argentina are to be given the chance to remove their men at Leith with the *Bahia Buen Suceso* or another ship. Poor Nick, no arrests, not at the moment anyway. I hope it means our own flight through Argentina tomorrow may prove uneventful.

24th March

BREAKFAST at 6.45. We started at 7. A rather grey windy day, quite cold. Rex, Mavis and Tony came to see us off, which really was kind of them. Thanks to Rex we whizzed through customs and got on the plane, rather, I fear, to the annoyance of others travelling on our flight. In fact half Stanley, if not half the Islands, seemed to be on the move. At Commodoro Rivadavia we made a hectic change of plans and changed from LADE to Aero Lineas as it meant a two-hours shorter flight. Only one stop at Bahia Blanca, a rather dull spot, and then B.A. Usual plastic sandwiches but at least a glass of white wine, instead of Fanta and dog-biscuits as on LADE.

Daniel (our agent) met us at B.A. So far, so good. No arrests, and although they examined our passports minutely, all went well. At B.A. we had to go from the Internal to the International Airport, quite some way, so we bought American papers, and one English, to see what the reports of the South Georgia goings-on were. Not very helpful.

It's all been blown up, the LADE incident in Stanley, where the office had rude words written on the windows. It has been reported as having the windows smashed, papers torn up, in fact the whole place wrecked, which is quite untrue.

Our Ambassador has apparently pleaded that we (U.K.) have blown up the South Georgia incident—"It's not really a grave matter at all". Dear me!

When we got to the International Airport we found that changing our tickets from Montevideo to Rio (our original plan) for tickets from B.A. to Rio practically constituted an offence. It took us two hours to get them changed. Daniel was marvellous and got frightfully up-stage and insisted that Daddy was "near the Minister" and name-dropped Costa Mendez or something along those lines, and eventually all was well.

It was incredibly hot and sticky in B.A. so it was quite a relief to board our plane, a Varig DC10, and relax.

We had a superb flight onwards, one stop at San Paulo, delicious dinner, and arrived at Rio at ten. Our luggage was the last to come off, and we had more forms to fill in than I've ever seen. Daddy's case had had the handle ripped off and one lock broken, which was a frightful nuisance. Eventually we found a taxi which took us to our hotel at Epenima, just out of Rio. It took half an hour and we saw the famous statue of Christ on the Cordovadas which is lit up at night, sadly rather shrouded in mist, but just visible.

We wondered how Cindy and Annie were, and what was going on down there. I wonder if Nick has taken them off. I feel much happier knowing he's down there keeping an eye on them.

Postscript

On 2nd April Argentine forces invaded the Falkland Islands, and the following day troops landed at Grytviken, South Georgia. Both at Port Stanley and at Grytviken the tiny Royal Marine garrisons surrendered to the superior Argentine forces after putting up stiff resistance. The B.A.S. scientists at Grytviken took refuge in the whalers' church and were eventually repatriated, but thirteen other B.A.S. men in South Georgia and Cindy and Annie remained until relieved by the British Task Force on 25th-26th April. Fears for the safety of those on South Georgia fortunately proved groundless, and they returned to Britain by way of Ascension Island on 14th May.

Comment

Captain Nicholas Barker, C.B.E., R.N.

I HAVE read Maria Buxton's diary with enthusiasm. Though I was present for many of the events which she describes and I frequently heard her either enthuse or criticize, her version of those events is delightful and all the more shaming, as far as I am concerned, that I did not always observe the beauty or the cruelty of the Antarctic ambience.

It was the greatest pleasure to have both the Buxtons on board for what we all thought was the final voyage of *Endurance* to the Antarctic. The ship's company, indeed the captain, had grown to love and admire their daughter Cindy and her film-making partner Annie Price, but until mid-1981 few had met the Buxton parents.

Everyone knew of Lord Buxton's support for the Falklands, the Islanders and the British presence in the South Atlantic; everyone in *Endurance* admired his public speeches and his enthusiasm for British aspirations in that area, and of course we all admired his consistent view that *Endurance* was doing a worthwhile job. He had become one of the great Antarctic enthusiasts and, in modern terms, a name to be linked with Scott, Shackleton, Fuchs and Laws.

So it was to our great pleasure when the Ministry of Defence approved the request for Lord and Lady Buxton to take passage in *Endurance* to see this incredible and indeed important part of the world at first hand and to learn of the international situation which existed before the start of the Falklands conflict.

I know that they were apprehensive of the living conditions, the weather, the movement of the ship and all the other unknowns which one faces when embarking upon a trip to the Antarctic. It was therefore with typical resolve that they accepted every invitation to venture ashore, often in appalling weather conditions. They were perfect guests as they never failed to be absorbed by the work of the ship, the efforts of the men and the ecology of the area. Lord Buxton educated us all with his knowledge of birds and Lady Buxton regularly reduced complicated situations to the sort of commonsense many of us had been trying to find for weeks. Lord Buxton's "attack" on the foam fire extinguisher will never be forgotten, and Lady Buxton's love of knitting when the going gets tough will also be remembered with affection.

This account of life in *Endurance*, life in the Antarctic and the situation throughout the area before the conflict, illustrates the human aspects of our daily work, while at the same time providing a touching account of communication between a devoted and close-knit family.

The rising crescendo of expectation when the family met on the beach at South Georgia is vividly expressed, and as does any sailor returning from sea, we knew how they all felt and what a surprise the Buxton parents would get when they saw the conditions in which those two brave girls were existing throughout the ever-changing and most inhospitable weather conditions of South Georgia.

This little book has given me great pleasure and I'm sure it will be one of the most amusing and affectionate accounts of recent events in that turbulent part of the globe. *Endurance* has much to thank the Buxtons for, and their presence gave an added dimension to an unforgettable trip to the ice.

FALKLAND ISLANDS

Port Stanley

CAPE HORN

DRAKE PASSAGE

SOUTH SHETLAND ISLANDS

Presidente Frei Base

Capitan Arturo Prat

N

Brabant Island

Palmer Base

Almirante Brown

Faraday Base

GRAHAM LAND

Adelaide Island

Rothera Base

Marguerite Bay

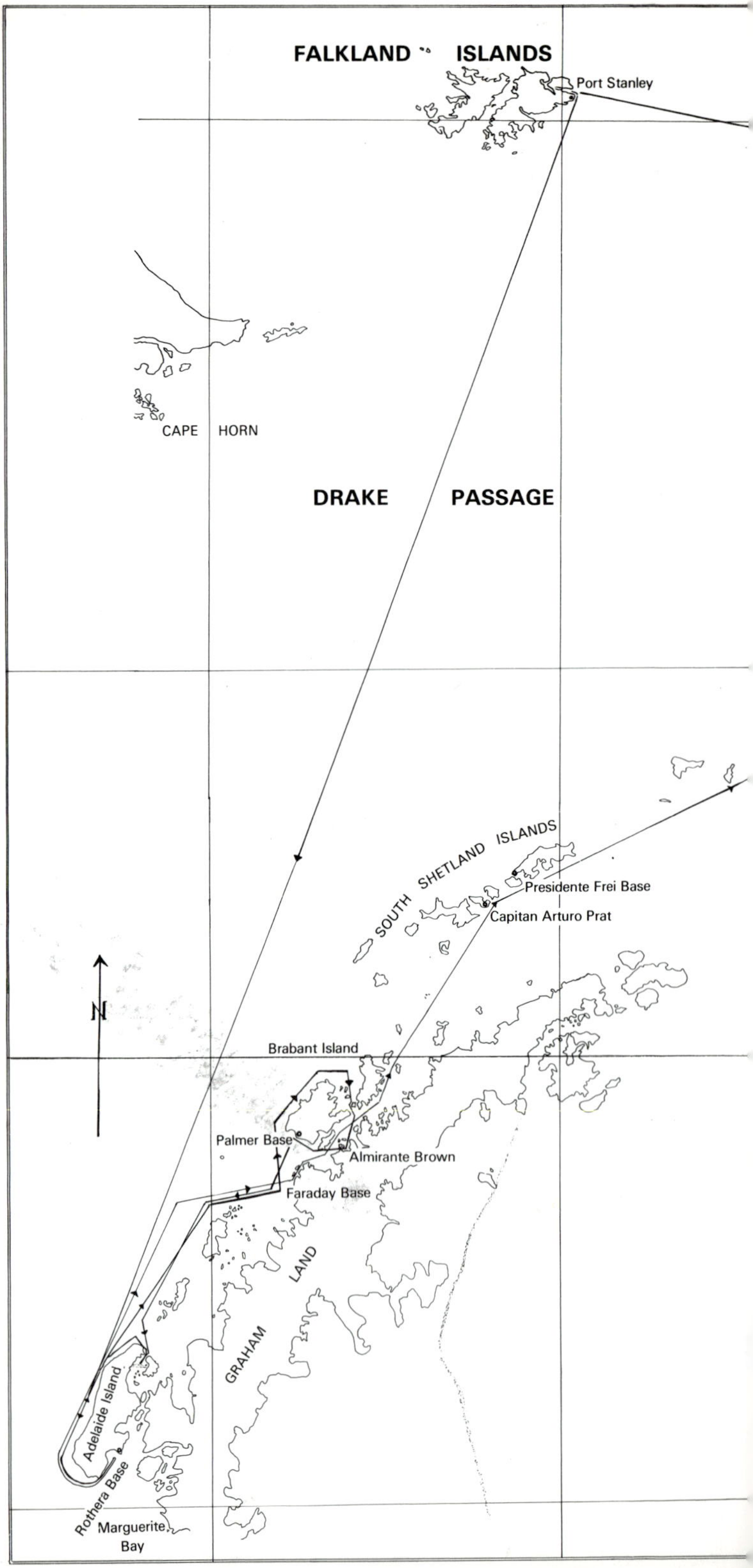